Thinking and Interacting Like a Leader

The TILL System for Effective Interpersonal Communication

Kim Sydow Campbell, PhD

Derrell Thomas Teaching Excellence Faculty Fellow

Culverhouse College of Commerce and Business Administration
at the University of Alabama

Tuscaloosa, Alabama

Parlay Press  **Chicago**

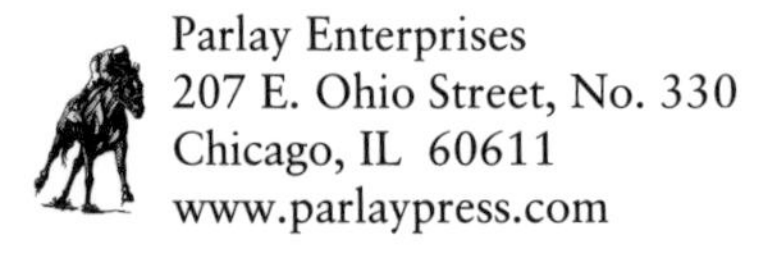

Parlay Enterprises
207 E. Ohio Street, No. 330
Chicago, IL 60611
www.parlaypress.com

Library of Congress Cataloging-in-Publication Data
Campbell, Kim Sydow, 1960-

Thinking and interacting like a leader: the TILL system for effective interpersonal communication / Kim Sydow Campbell
Includes bibliographical references and index.
ISBN 0–9767180–2–2

For Kevin

Do not ask about the harvest; ask about the tilling.

-Chinese Proverb

Contents

Illustrations

TABLES

FIGURES

EXHIBITS

Preface

This book is designed to help managers become better leaders. By virtue of their organizational position, managers have "position" power over some members of their organization. They can hire and fire, sanction a bonus or promotion, and assign both desirable and undesirable tasks. However, managers who are great leaders have an additional source of power that is not related to their official position within the organization. Great leaders influence people through "personal" power—their knowledge and behavior. The system of effective leadership communication introduced in this book is designed to increase your own personal power. In essence, this system focuses on interpersonal communication skills. However, you'll see that the system addresses management situations including written and electronic, as well as face-to-face, communication.

This book is designed to be used and not simply read. This may seem obvious to those who picked up the book because they seek to develop their own leadership skills. But even for those who are simply seeking a better understanding of the role of communication in leadership, active engagement is essential. My training as a linguist taught me that the only way to truly understand anything abstract is to apply it to concrete examples.

I have provided many example messages from leaders throughout the book. Some of these are dialogue adapted from popular films. Although I have included enough context to show how those dialogues demonstrate the principles being discussed, you may find watching the films beneficial—especially if you've never seen them.

There are many people at the University of Alabama who influenced the ideas presented here. First, I owe my students in the Master of Arts program in Management over the past six years a tremendous debt. They challenged me to help them make sense out of the role of communication in leadership. They also provided me with a wealth of real-world examples of leaders communicating with organizational members and interesting sample answers to the exercises in some chapters. I appreciate their intellectual curiosity, diligent work ethic, and commitment to elevate the profession of management.

Second, I owe my colleague, Diane Johnson, for helping me begin thinking about language and leadership. Finally, this book would not be what it is without the influence of my doctoral students, Charles White and Rita Durant, who have been both students and teachers along the path that led to the development of this book. They are also both exceptional human beings.

I want to thank Frank Parker at Parlay, who was the best mentor any graduate student could have found and is now the best editor anyone could want.

Finally, I want to say how deeply I appreciate Sean's willingness to allow mom to shut her office door and work with minimal interruption.

1
Introduction

To help you understand where we're headed in this book, let's consider two leaders from the film *Crimson Tide*. Both are male Navy officers on a submarine, the *U.S.S. Alabama*. The ship has been ordered to get into position to launch nuclear missiles against Russia. The crew is highly stressed while waiting to receive orders. First, we'll concentrate on Executive Officer Hunter (played by Denzel Washington), who witnesses a fight between two seamen and then confronts one of them named Rivetti (Exhibit 1a).

Hunter: Rivetti, what's up?
Rivetti: Sorry, sir. . . . just a difference of opinion that got out of hand.
Hunter: What about?
Rivetti: I'd rather just forget about it. [Sir].
Hunter: I don't [care] what you'd rather forget about.
Rivetti [pause]: Well I said the Kirby silver surfer was the only real silver surfer. And that the Mobius silver surfer was shit. And Benefield's a big Mobius fan. And uh things got out of hand.
Hunter: Rivetti, you're a supervisor. You can get a commission . . .
Rivetti: It'll never happen again. [Sir].
Hunter: It better not. . . I see this kind of nonsense, I'm gonna write you up. You understand? . . .
Rivetti: Yes, sir.
Hunter: You have to set an example even in the face of stupidity. . . . Everybody who reads comic books knows . . . Kirby silver surfer is the only real silver surfer. . . . am I right or wrong?
Rivetti [laughing]: You're right, sir.

Exhibit 1a. Interaction between a leader (Executive Officer Hunter) and organizational member (Seaman Rivetti) in *Crimson Tide*.

Next, we'll observe Captain Ramsey (played by Gene Hackman) later on the same day in a dialogue that involves Hunter and the entire crew of the submarine.

Ramsey [to Hunter]: Feels like the whole crew needs a kick in the ass.
Hunter: Or a pat on the back, sir. [pause] I just witnessed a fight down in crew's mess. . . . I think the men are . . . . uh a bit on edge . . . . Morale seems to be a bit low.
Ramsey: Well you seem to have the pulse of the men. . . . [communicating over intercom to ship's crew] May I have your attention please. Mr. Hunter has brought it to my attention that morale may be a bit low. . . . [pause while look-

ing at Hunter] So I suggest this. Any crew member who feels he can't handle the situation can leave the ship right now. [pause] Gentleman, . . . war is imminent. [pause] This is the captain. [pause] That is all.
Hunter: Very inspiring, sir.

Exhibit 1b. Interaction between a leader (Captain Ramsey) and organizational members, including Executive Officer Hunter, in *Crimson Tide*.

When comparing Hunter and Ramsey, most readily agree Hunter is the more effective leader. Hunter has somehow made a personal "connection" with the seaman despite the fact that he is absolutely clear about who is in charge, what the seaman did wrong, and how he should act in the future. Effective leaders intuitively know how to achieve these apparently incompatible goals. In short, this book shows you what's behind their magic—how to think (T) and interact (I) like (L) a leader (L): TILL.

In the remainder of this chapter, I'll help you understand how and why TILL is needed by providing some background material on communication, leadership, and management.

Communication Satisfaction

Employees' satisfaction with communication in their workplace has been clearly connected to several vital signs of an organization's health. For example, employees who are satisfied with communication are more productive in and satisfied with their jobs. In addition, employee communication satisfaction is related to organizational performance:

> Companies with the highest levels of effective communication experienced a 26 percent total return to shareholders from 1998 to 2002, compared to a –15 percent return experienced by firms that communicate least effectively. (Watson Wyatt, 2005)

Not surprisingly, employees' satisfaction with communication is determined largely by the quality of the relationships between organizational leaders and their employees.

At least since the 1970s, we've known that managers spend a great deal of their time in face-to-face interaction with subordinates as part of their organizational role. Unfortunately, one study at an international hotel chain found that, of all the interactions that pitched employees into bad moods, the most frequent was talking to someone in management. About nine out of ten times, interactions with bosses led to bad feelings (e.g., frustration, disappointment, anger, sadness, disgust, or hurt). Manager-subordinate interactions caused the employees distress more often than did customers, work pressure, company policies, or personal problems. The magnitude of the problem: One study reported that 60% of American workers found interacting with their boss stressful.

Because of this, managers have been advised to develop higher quality relationships with more members of their organization in order to increase employee satisfaction. Unfortunately, leaders' and their members' evaluations of the quality of their relationships don't match. Leaders consistently overestimate the quality of their relationships with members. In a nutshell, the primary solution to improving employee communication satisfaction is better leader-member relationships, but leaders rarely recognize the need for improvement.

To make matters worse, even if leaders recognize the need for improved relationships with members, many lack the needed communication skills. In a 2001 survey sponsored by the Academy of Management and reported in *Training* magazine, Martin Delahoussaye found that leaders' actual communication skills don't match those they need to succeed: Of all required leadership skills, communication is of most value to organizations but showed the largest gap between importance to the organization and current competency.

To sum up, we know that leaders must be expert communicators in order to build better relationships with members and influence communication satisfaction (as well as productivity, job satisfaction, job performance, and organizational effectiveness), but that they rarely are. You saw how easy it was to recognize a good leader in Exhibits 1a and 1b from *Crimson Tide*. The goal of TILL is to show you precisely how to improve your relationships with members by thinking like a leader through a set of questions about the management situation and then using your answers to interact like a leader. In the following section, I will cover some foundational concepts related to management and leadership.

Management or Leadership?

Henry Mintzberg provided a definition of management based on the actual behavior of managers; he identified ten managerial roles within three categories (1975). In the category of **Interpersonal Relationship-Builder**, a manager serves as:

1. Figurehead (e.g., greeting touring dignitaries or taking a client to lunch)
2. Leader (e.g., hiring or motivating subordinates)

3. Liaison (e.g., meeting with peer-managers within the organization or in similar organizations)

In the category of **Informational Nerve Center,** a manager serves as:

4. Monitor (e.g., listening to gossip or initiating speculation)
5. Disseminator (e.g., passing along information to subordinates)
6. Spokesperson (e.g., suggesting a product innovation to a supplier or reporting productivity to superiors)

Finally, in the category of **Decision-Maker,** a manager serves as:

7. Entrepreneur (e.g., developing a new public relations campaign or improving the cash position of the unit)
8. Disturbance Handler (e.g., responding to the bankruptcy of a major customer)
9. Resource Allocator (e.g., approving funds for a new software application)
10. Negotiator (e.g., negotiating a new union contract)

Within Mintzberg's definition, "leadership" is one component of "management." This is the perspective I take here. I distinguish "managing" from "leading" in a straightforward way: Managing requires a focus on tasks, while leading requires a focus on relationships with the people involved in those tasks. One of the most constructive features of TILL is that management and leadership are included within a single communication system. I'll have more to say about this in the following chapter.

For now, it may be helpful to compare two memos written by a recruiting director within a human resource department to hiring managers in his organization. In Exhibit 1c, the writer is disseminating information about recruiting costs. His focus on tasks makes this memo a management message. We might describe the memo as "straightforward" or "impersonal." My point here is not to critique this memo but simply to provide a clear example of a management-oriented message focusing on tasks.

TO: Managers
FROM: Bill Stone, Recruiting Director
DATE: 11/2/06
RE: Recruiting Costs

Several managers have questioned me about the costs to recruit. I thought I would use this memo to educate you on the costs incurred in the hiring process.

* Newspaper ads minimally cost approximately $100/wk per ad. Our most expensive ads cost $250/wk per ad. So, for a month's worth of newspaper advertising we have to spend minimally $400 per ad; maximum $1000 per ad.

* Internet recruiting sites (Hot Jobs) cost approximately $100/month per ad. Specialty sites (Dice.com) cost approximately $200/month per ad.

* Our applicant tracking system, which processes all resumes we receive (approximately 500 per month), costs $600/month.

For the above reasons, it is extremely important that our budget and time resources in recruiting be used as efficiently as possible.

Exhibit 1c. A management message focused on tasks.

Now compare the message in Exhibit 1d. We might call this memo "persuasive" or "personal" because the writer focuses not only on "what" (i.e., tasks related to recruiting support) but also on "who." The writer is trying to enhance his relationship with the audience by demonstrating that he not only appreciates their input but has taken it seriously. His interpersonal focus on relationships makes this memo a leadership message.

TO: Managers
FROM: Bill Stone, Human Resource Director
DATE: 7/28/06
RE: Results of the Recruiting Survey

In February, we sent out a survey of our recruiting process to get ideas and suggestions for improving our service to you. Thank you all for taking the time to respond to the survey. The information we gained was very helpful.

Many of you said you have been happy with the results you have seen and have been glad to no longer have to manage recruiting yourselves. The positive feedback was very encouraging. However, now that we have some basic processes in place, we realize that improvement is the next step. Based on your responses, we will be taking several steps this year to make our service even better:

* Working to decrease the time to fill a position by using the Human Resource Assistant for administrative areas of recruiting.

* Researching and implementing more automation to further decrease the time to fill a position. Through technology we hope to have a better system of handling candidate flow and reporting of recruiting activities.

* Updating the career section of our organizational website and increasing recruiting resources available there.

* Communicating more proactively with managers to determine departmental forecasting and goals. I hope to meet with all of you periodically to discuss your plans.

Exhibit 1d. A leadership message focused on relationships.

There is nothing inherently good or bad about either a management (task-oriented) or a leadership (relationship-oriented) message. Table 1a lists the terminology used by the most influential leadership researchers to differentiate between task-focus and relationship-focus. Throughout this book, we will see evidence that the most effective leaders focus on both tasks and relationships and that they choose their focus based on the needs of their members as well as those of their organization.

Task-Focus for Management	Relationship-Focus for Leadership	Leadership Model
Production-orientation, technical aspects, output, employee as tool	Employee-oriented, interest in individuality and personal needs	Michigan Leadership Studies
Initiating structure, task-oriented, goal achievement orientation	Consideration, sensitive to subordinates, respectful, trust	Ohio State Leadership Studies
Hierarchical, centralized, close control of people	Self-control, creativity, self-direction, motivation	McGregor's Theory X
Authoritarian, position-based power, theory X	Democratic, relationship-based power, motivation, theory Y	Tannenbaum-Schmidt Continuum
Concern for production	Concern for people	Blake & McCanse's Leadership Grid
Task-structure, clear procedures and methods of evaluation	Leader-member relations, friendliness, cooperation, enthusiasm	Fiedler's Contingency Theory
Organize and define roles, clear goals and procedures	Communication, socio-emotional support, active listening	Hersey Blanchard Tri-Dimensional
Structuring behavior, clarify task and path to goal	Consideration behavior	House-Mitchell Path-Goal Theory

Table 1a. Task-focus vs. relationship-focus.

In sum, managing requires a focus on tasks associated with the roles of informational nerve-center and decision-maker, while leading requires a focus on relationships with the people involved in those tasks. The importance of interpersonal skills in establishing productive workplace relationships is one reason why "emotional intelligence," or "EQ," has become such a hot topic within the business world (Goleman, Boyatzis & McKee 2002).

Leadership Communication

Many people claim persuasion is the key to leadership communication. For instance, in *The Language of Leadership*, Roger Soder demonstrates the central role of persuasion in effective leadership from the ancient Greeks through modern times. He argues that the ability to persuade is the reason leaders have followers. His book emphasizes persuasive language use by charismatic public leaders like Winston Churchill.

As another example, in *The Art of Framing: Managing the Language of Leadership*, Gail Fairhurst and Robert Sarr emphasize the language of everyday leaders in organizations and argue that their effectiveness lies in their ability to manage meaning by "framing": a quality of communication that causes others to accept one meaning (i.e., the leader's) over another.

Despite the differences in their approaches to leadership communication, both of these analysts assume effective leaders expertly control others in order to manipulate (i.e., "persuade," "influence," or "direct") them to achieve the leader's or organization's goals. However, it's hard for me to believe that the managers in the hotel chain mentioned earlier just needed to be more "persuasive" when interacting with their employees in order to create better feelings. While persuasion is an important skill for leaders, it is not sufficient—nor even the most important skill—for leading the people in an organization. Rather, I showed you above that leading requires a focus on relationships, which are rarely enhanced by any form of manipulation. The TILL system is different from most approaches to leadership communication because it provides an emotionally intelligent system for managing relationships.

Preview of the TILL System

In Chapters 2 through 6, you learn a structured method for thinking like a leader when you anticipate interacting with a member. (We'll use the term "member" instead of "subordinate" throughout this book.) The TILL system guides your thinking about the management situation by asking you to answer four questions:

- What is the organizational purpose driving you to communicate with the member—and how urgent is your need to act? (Chapter 2)
- Is the member one of your in-group? (Chapter 3)
- How will your message affect the member's ego needs? (Chapter 4)
- How will your message affect the member's autonomy needs? (Chapter 5)

In Chapter 6, we'll review the core ideas from the chapters on thinking like a leader.

Once you've learned the key to thinking like a leader, Chapters 7 through 10 teach you strategies for interacting like a leader. You will learn to choose from one of four sets of communication tactics in order to manage rapport with organizational members:

- Going ON RECORD PLAINLY (Chapter 7)
- Going OFF RECORD (Chapter 8)

- Tending Ego Needs by Going ON RECORD POLITELY (Chapter 9)
- Tending Autonomy Needs by Going ON RECORD POLITELY (Chapter 10)

In Chapter 11, we'll review these chapters on interacting like a leader. In the final chapter, we will return to the dialogue from *Crimson Tide* (Exhibits 1a and 1b) so that you can use the TILL system to understand the "magic" of leadership.

TILLing is hard work. To get the most out of this book, you must complete the exercises at the end of each chapter. Each application exercise asks you to apply the concepts from that chapter in an analysis of leader-member interaction. The chapters are interrelated and should be completed in the order in which they are arranged. The readings are relatively brief because you should spend more time thinking about and discussing the applications of TILL than reading about them if you are serious about improving your leadership skills.

Definitions

Before closing this first chapter, I want to provide the fundamental definitions we will adopt in the TILL system for effective interpersonal communication.

What is communication? The answer to this question is simple: Communication means shared meaning. For example, you create shared meaning when you use words (or nonverbal cues like eye contact) your audience understands. Saying (or writing) "cat" to another speaker of English means I've created some shared meaning—both of us share some meaning for "cat." However, the more my audience knows about me and my experiences with cats, the more meaning we will have in common when I use that word—i.e., the more I communicate. In other words, there is more shared meaning between my husband and me when I say "cat" than there is between you and me.

What is management and leadership communication? The answer to this question is also simple: Both management and leadership communication mean facilitating shared meaning in order to meet organizational goals. Let's go back to the examples from *Crimson Tide* to see how managers and leaders communicate (i.e., facilitate shared meaning). In Exhibit 1a, Hunter makes sure the seaman who had been involved in the fight shares Hunter's meaning for "consequences of inappropriate behavior in the future." Hunter makes clear that the seaman's behavior was inappropriate and that he will suffer serious consequences if it happens again. Thus, Hunter acts as a manager focused on tasks by informing and directing the member about appropriate behavior in their organization.

In the same dialogue, Hunter shows he shares the meaning of "Kirby silver surfer" with the seaman—even though this comic book lore is outside the realm of their organizational roles. Hunter sides with the seaman's position on the identity of the "real" silver surfer. Thus, Hunter acts as a leader focused on relationships by showing the value he places on the seaman as an individual and extending the bounds of their relationship.

My position in this book is that management communication and leadership communication are related but different. "To manage" means to facilitate shared meaning about tasks, whereas "to lead" means to facilitate shared meaning about relationships. Nevertheless, we'll see in the following chapter that the most effective individuals in organizations engage in both management and leadership communication.

The Bottom Line

In Chapter 1, we've discussed the importance of employee communication satisfaction in successful organizations. I have presented leadership as one component of management. While managers focus on organizational tasks, leaders focus on organizational relationships. To develop productive relationships with members of their organizations, leaders need excellent communication skills. Unfortunately, most leaders do not have such skills—and what's worse—they don't recognize that they lack them. The TILL system is different from most approaches to leadership communication because it focuses on the ability to manage relationships in an emotionally intelligent way based on the management situation. The goal in the remainder of the book is to show you precisely how to improve your relationships with members by thinking like a leader through a set of questions about the management situation and then using your answers to interact like a leader.

While defining management or leadership communication is simple enough, it requires more than a definition to truly understand it. It is important that you attempt the application exercises at the end of the chapter in order to grasp what you have been reading about. "Correct" answers are less important than reflection and experience at this point. You may also want to investigate the additional readings to pursue the ideas in this chapter in greater detail.

Further Reading

Delahoussaye, M. (2001) Leadership in the 21st century: Part one. *Training*, August: 50-59.

Delahoussaye, M. (2001) Leadership in the 21st century: Part two. *Training*, September: 60-72.

These two articles provide the details of an extensive survey of training programs in leadership development and establish the importance of communication skills.

Bass, B. M. (1990) Bass & Stogdill's Handbook of Leadership Theory, Research, & Managerial Applications, 3rd ed. New York: The Free Press.

Dubrin, A. J. (2003) *Leadership: Research Findings, Practice, and Skills*, 4th ed. Boston: Houghton Mifflin.

These two books are comprehensive treatments of leadership. Both include some discussion of the role of communication for leaders.

Applications

1A. Read Exhibit 1e from the film *12 Angry Men*. At this point in the movie, the twelve-man jury has entered the jury room to begin their deliberation to determine the guilt or innocence of a man accused of stabbing his father to death. The judge has instructed the jury that if there is a reasonable doubt, they must declare the accused not guilty; if not, then the accused must be found guilty. In addition, the judge instructs them that their decision must be unanimous. Pay special attention to the behaviors of the Foreman (played by Lee J. Cobb) and Juror #8 (played by Henry Fonda). Use Table 1a to categorize their behaviors. Based on your observation of the communication between these two characters, does either of them appear to be a leader? Give two specific pieces of evidence to support your answer.

Foreman: You gentlemen can handle this any way you want to. If we want to discuss it first and then vote, that's one way. Or we can vote right now. [Several jurors suggest voting before any further discussion.] All those voting guilty raise your hands. [Jurors # 3, #7, #10, and #12 put their hands up instantly. The Foreman and Jurors #2, #4, #5, and #6 follow a second later. Then Juror #11 raises his hand and a moment later Juror #9 puts his hand up.] Eight—nine—ten—eleven—that's eleven for guilty. Okay. Not guilty? [Juror #8's hand goes up. All turn to look at him.]

Juror #3: You're in left field! . . . [rises and looks at Juror #8] Do you really believe he's not guilty?

Juror #8: [quietly] I don't know.. . .

Juror #3: I never saw a guiltier man in my life. [sitting again]

Juror #8: What does a guilty man look like? Are we to vote on his face?

Juror #3: The man's a dangerous killer. You could see it.
Juror #8: Where do you look to see if a man is a killer?. . .
Tell me what the facial characteristics of a killer are. . . . .
Juror #10: [rising and looking at Juror #8] Do you believe that stupid story he told?
Juror #8: I don't know whether I believe it or not . . . It's not so easy for me to raise my hand and send a boy off to die without talking about it first. . . .
Foreman: He's still just as guilty, whether it's an easy vote or a hard vote.
Juror #7: I think the guy's guilty. You couldn't change my mind if you talked for a hundred years. . . .
Juror #8: Look—this boy's been kicked around all his life. . . . living in a slum—his mother dead since he was nine. . . . He's a tough, angry kid. . . . I think maybe we owe him a few words.
Juror # 4: If we're going to discuss this case, . . . let's discuss the facts.
Foreman: I think that's a good point. We have a job to do. Let's do it.

Exhibit 1e. Interaction among jurors in *12 Angry Men*.

1B. Read Exhibit 1f from the film *Miracle*, which recounts the story of the U.S. hockey team's miracle performance during the 1982 Olympic Games under coach Herb Brooks (played by Kurt Russell). Then read Exhibit 1g from the film *Hoosiers*, about a high school basketball team in small-town Indiana led by Coach Dale (played by Gene Hackman). Use Table 1a to compare the behaviors of the two coaches. Do the coaches act as managers or leaders in each situation? Give specific evidence to support your answer.

Brooks: This is unbelievable. You guys are playing like this is some throw-away game up in Rochester. Who we playing, Ramer?
Mike Ramsey: Sweden.
Brooks: You're damn right! In the Olympics!!
Brooks: [to McClanahan] Put your gear on! [repeats his order]
Rob McClanahan: The Doc told me I can't play.
Brooks: Yeah, yeah, I know. You gotta bad bruise. . . . Put your street clothes on 'cause I got no time for quitters.. . . Bruise on the leg is a hellava long way from the heart, you candy ass.
Rob McClanahan: What'd you call me?
Brooks: You heard me.
Rob McClanahan: You want me to play? . . . Is that what you want?!
Brooks: I want you to be a hockey player!!
Rob McClanahan: I am a hockey player!! . . .
Brooks: [to Assistant Coach, Craig Patrick, as he leaves the locker room] Think that'll get 'em goin'?
Craig Patrick: Oh, yeah..

Exhibit 1f. Halftime interaction between Coach Brooks and hockey players in *Miracle*.

Coach Dale: We've been all over this before. Their top player is Boyle, number 15. He averages about 20 points a game. Buddy, you gotta stick right with him. No inside penetration. Shut down those passing lanes. And you gotta play tough off those boards -- negate their height advantage.
Official: Hickory, it's time to take the floor.
Colin Butcher: I'll get preacher.
Coach Dale: Okay. Well we're way past big speech time. I wanna thank you for the last few months. It's been very special for me. Anybody have anything they wanna say.
Merle: Yeah. Let's win this one for all the small schools that never had a chance to get here.
Coach Dale: Okay.
Buddy: Let's win for coach. You got us here.
Coach Dale: Thank you.
[The Preacher leads the team in a prayer.]
Coach Dale: [huddling with the team] I love you guys.
Coach and Players: [shouting] TEAM!

Exhibit 1g. Locker room interaction between Coach Dale and basketball players in *Hoosiers*.

2

Organizational Purpose and Manager Actions

In this chapter, you will learn to recognize the different organizational purposes that drive managers to act by creating messages for members. You may have learned about rhetorical purpose in university classes that taught writing or speaking. For instance, you might remember that in freshman English you had to write essays with different rhetorical purposes (i.e., narration, description, process, argumentation, etc.). I will use management research to categorize the rhetorical purposes that drive managers to communicate with organizational members.

The Competing Values Framework

Robert Quinn and his colleagues developed the COMPETING VALUES FRAMEWORK by identifying the four overarching organizational values that drive managers' behavior:

1. To consolidate internal organizational processes
2. To maximize organizational output
3. To adapt the organization to change
4. To build organizational commitment and trust

These are shown in the shaded upper triangles in each quadrant of Figure 2a. Experts agree that the most effective managers are those who are influenced by multiple values—even though those values sometimes conflict (or "compete") for the manager's attention. For instance, the sales manager whose behavior is influenced only by his desire to increase profit percentage (i.e., maximize output) is going to be less effective than the manager who is influenced by (a) his desire to build trust (e.g., by following through on his promise for a new commission structure), (b) his desire to adapt to change (e.g., learning all he can about a new competitor in his market), and (c) his desire to maximize output (e.g., increase profit).

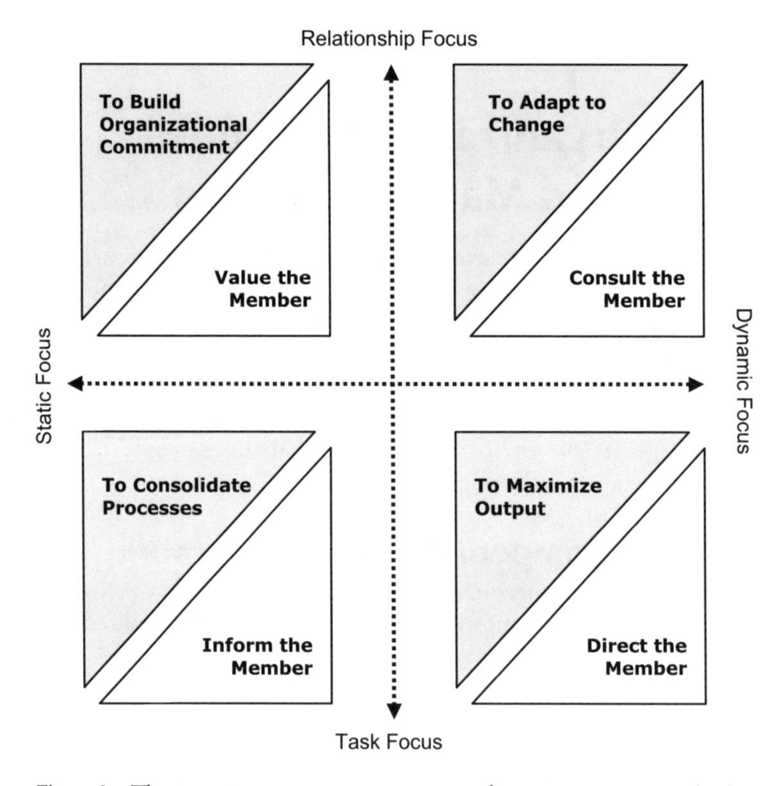

Figure 2a. The COMPETING VALUES FRAMEWORK of management communication.

Communication researchers have extended the COMPETING VALUES FRAMEWORK to argue that effective management messages must reflect multiple values (i.e., competing goals) to be effective. (See the unshaded triangles in Figure 2a.) Those researchers explain that a presentation that is highly informative (see the lower left quadrant) but does not actively involve the audience (see the upper right quadrant) may be so boring and monotonic as to receive virtually no consideration from the audience.

Let's look at examples of messages reflecting each of the four value quadrants. All of the examples are memos written by a recruiting director within the human resources department to hiring managers in his organization.

Informing Members

Read the memo shown in Exhibit 2a.

TO: Managers
FROM: Bill Stone, Recruiting Director
DATE: 11/2/06
RE: Recruiting Costs

Several managers have questioned me about the costs to recruit. I thought I would use this memo to educate you on the costs incurred in the hiring process.

* Newspaper Ads minimally cost approximately $100/wk per ad. Our most expensive ads cost $250/wk per ad. So, for a month's worth of newspaper advertising we have to spend minimally $400 per ad; maximum $1000 per ad.

* Internet recruiting sites (Hot Jobs) cost approximately $100/month per ad. Specialty sites (Dice.com) cost approximately $200/month per ad.

* Our applicant tracking system, which processes all resumes we receive (approximately 500 per month), costs $600/month.

For the above reasons, it is extremely important that our budget and time resources in recruiting be used as efficiently as possible.

Exhibit 2a. A message used to consolidate internal processes of the organization by informing members.

This memo contains a message from a manager with the primary goal of informing members involved in recruiting, about the costs associated with hiring (lower left quadrant of Figure 2a.).

Directing Members

The memo shown in Exhibit 2b was written by the same HR director to the same organizational members, but with a different organizational purpose. This memo has the goal of directing members' behavior and expectations about recruiting. While the manager also informs his audience in this message, the information conveyed is subordinate to his primary goal of directing members' behavior in order to maximize efficiency (lower right quadrant of Figure 2a).

TO: Managers
FROM: Bill Stone, Recruiting Director
DATE: 8/22/06
RE: Recruiting Protocol

In order to serve you best, it is important all managers follow certain protocols set by the recruiting department in regard to hiring. For your part, we need the following:

(1) Before submitting a job requisition, please use as much due diligence as needed to fully understand the specifics of the job and that the position is a viable and available position. In several recent cases, we have recruited for a position for weeks (or even months) only to be told to stop interviewing candidates. Later we were told that the manager or department was never really sure they would fill the job. Obviously, much time and money can be saved if departments are committed to hiring before we proceed to recruit and interview applicants.
(2) If an unforeseen change occurs either in the requirements for an open job or in whether the job will actually continue to be viable, keep us in the loop! Sometimes a change cannot be avoided, but the sooner we know, the sooner we will reallocate resources to where they are needed.
(3) When you come to us with a request to begin recruiting, expect us to ask questions about the position and your department. This is not to question your need, but rather to make sure that our employment practices are compliant with our policy, as well as state and federal laws.

Exhibit 2b. A message used to maximize output of the organization by directing members.

Consulting Members

Consider the memo shown in Exhibit 2c. This memo contains a message from a manager with the goal of consulting organizational members about recruiting in order to adapt the organization to future change (upper right quadrant of Figure 2a).

TO: Managers
FROM: Bill Stone, Recruiting Director
DATE: 4/16/06
RE: Recruiting Survey

Do you have ideas and suggestions for improving our recruiting service? Please take a few minutes to complete the survey attached to this memo.

Exhibit 2c. A message used to adapt the organization to change by consulting members.

Valuing Members

As our final example, read the memo reproduced in Exhibit 2d. This memo contains a message from a manager with the goal of valuing members in order to build trust and organizational commitment. While the manager also informs his audience in this message, the information is subordinate to his primary goal of building commitment (upper left quadrant of Figure 2a).

Interestingly, these four categories of the COMPETING VALUES FRAMEWORK (Figure 2a) coincide with major categories of SPEECH ACTS recognized by linguists (Searle 1976). Linguists have long known that words can be used to *do* things as well as *say* things. For example, when a priest says *I now pronounce you husband and wife*, the priest is actually causing the two people to become married. Likewise, when a dignitary says *I name this the Good Ship Lollipop*, the dignitary is actually causing the ship to be named. And so on. Linguists have thus categorized speech acts into a handful of basic types which bear a correspondence to the four cells of the COMPETING VALUES FRAMEWORK.

- First, informing a member involves an act called a "representative," in which a leader asserts the truth of some proposition (e.g., *Our most expensive ads cost $250/wk* in Exhibit 2a).
- Second, directing a member involves an act called a "directive," in which a leader prescribes a member's future behavior (e.g., *If an unforeseen change occurs, keep us in the loop* in Exhibit 2b).
- Third, consulting a member involves an act called a "question," in which a leader attempts to elicit information from a member (e.g., *Do you have ideas and suggestions for improving our recruiting service?* in Exhibit 2c).
- Fourth, valuing a member involves either an act called an "expressive," in which the leader makes his or her emotional state known to the

member (e.g., *Thank you all for taking the time to respond to the survey* in Exhibit 2d) or an act called a "commissive," in which the leader commits to some future behavior on behalf of the member (e.g., *we will be taking several steps this year to make our service even better* in Exhibit 2d).

TO: Managers
FROM: Bill Stone, Human Resource Director
DATE: 7/28/06
RE: Results of the Recruiting Survey

In February, we sent out a survey of our recruiting process to get ideas and suggestions for improving our service to you. Thank you all for taking the time to respond to the survey. The information we gained was very helpful.

Many of you said you have been happy with the results you have seen and have been glad to no longer have to manage recruiting yourselves. The positive feedback was very encouraging. However, now that we have some basic processes in place, we realize that improvement is the next step. Based on your responses, we will be taking several steps this year to make our service even better:

* Working to decrease the time to fill a position using the Human Resource Assistant for administrative areas of recruiting.
* Researching and implementing more automation to further decrease the time to fill a position. Through technology we hope to have a better system of handling candidate flow and reporting of recruiting activities.
* Updating the career section of our organizational website and increasing recruiting resources available there.
* Communicating more proactively with managers to determine departmental forecasting and goals. I hope to meet with all of you periodically to discuss your plans.

Exhibit 2d. A message used to build commitment to the organization by valuing members.

Figure 2b captures the correspondence between specific speech acts and specific quadrants in the competing values framework. This correspondence will help us develop communication strategies in Chapter 7.

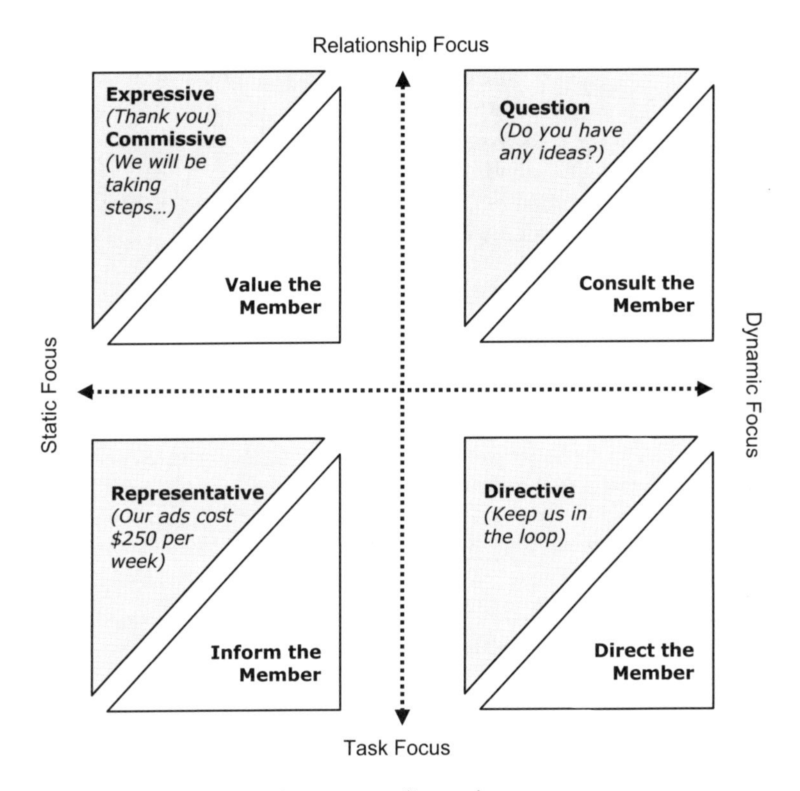

Figure 2b. SPEECH ACT categories corresponding to the COMPETING VALUES FRAMEWORK of management communication.

Conclusions about Manager Actions

Not surprisingly, individual managers show strong preferences for values within a single quadrant. It's fairly easy to see how a manager can get stuck in the bottom quadrants of Figure 2a, acting exclusively by informing and directing members because of a focus on consolidating processes and maximizing output. Because of the focus on tasks, that manager might be called a "transactional" leader or merely a "manager," or even a lowly "bureaucrat." In contrast, a manager who actively values and consults members could be called a "transformational" leader or an "emotionally intelligent" leader (one with "EQ") because leading requires a relationship focus (top two quadrants of Figure 2a).

An effective manager, however, will be both "transactional" (task-focused) and "transformational" (relationship-focused) with each member of the organization. In other words, the best managers are not stuck in any one quadrant of

Figure 2a. For instance, a manager might be predisposed to communicate in a way that emphasizes adaptation to change—she constantly solicits ideas from members within her organization. Although her communication goal may be laudable and sometimes effective, research tells us that managers who are able to focus on all four value quadrants achieve higher levels of performance. If this manager wants her members to be top performers, she must know not only when to solicit ideas but also when to set standards.

Regardless of the medium used to convey it, any message from a manager to a member can also be described within the COMPETING VALUES FRAMEWORK. Consider the following dialogue.

Leader: Where are we on the system upgrade plan?
Member: We had hoped to finish our analysis last week but we are concerned about potential impacts to the security team. Bill noticed . . .
Leader: [interrupting] Our report has to be ready next week.
Member: I think we need more information before we recommend changes to the system.
Leader: More information won't make this problem easier to solve.

Exhibit 2e. A problematic interaction between manager and member.

The manager's actions in this interchange rate high on directing (lower right quadrant of Figure 2a) and informing (lower left quadrant), but low on consulting (upper right quadrant) and valuing the member (upper left quadrant). This type of interchange exemplifies those that lead to a member's dissatisfaction with internal communication. If the need to act is truly urgent, then the manager may be forgiven for ignoring the upper quadrants of the competing values model. However, when enough of these interchanges occur, we can be virtually certain that both employee communication satisfaction and the quality of the manager's relationship with the member are low. I'll have more to say about relationship quality in Chapter 3.

The Bottom Line: Thinking Like a Leader

For now, it's important to understand that managers become more effective not only by informing and directing organizational members but also by valuing and consulting them. This range of actions is what makes an individual a leader in addition to a manager. To think like a leader requires that you answer the question: *What is the organizational purpose driving you to communicate with the member—and how urgent is your need to act?*

Further Reading

Quinn, R.E. (1991) Beyond Rational Management: Mastering the Paradoxes and Competing Demands of High Performance. San Francisco: Jossey-Bass.
If you would like to know more about the COMPETING VALUES FRAMEWORK within the field of management, I suggest this 1991 book.

Quinn, R. E., Hildebrandt, H. W., Rogers, P. S., and Thompson, M. P. (1991) A competing values framework for analyzing presentational communication in management contexts. *Journal of Business Communication*, 28: 213-232.
This article explains the extension of that framework to the creation of management messages and is written for an academic audience.

Applications

2A. To practice recognizing and categorizing the organizational goals and intended actions of leaders, read the letter in Exhibit 2f. The author of this message is a publication manager who supervises the paid professional staff producing research journals headed by Volunteer Editors (with fulltime academic jobs). The manager sent this letter because of serious delays in getting journals produced and mailed. What is the primary organizational goal driving the writer to create this message? Is the letter effective? Does the writer primarily inform, direct, consult, or value the audience? Give two specific pieces of evidence that support your answer.

Dear Volunteer Editor,

I am writing to you to give you an update on the status of our journal schedules for this year's issues. Some of you may have already been contacted individually by your staff editor regarding our ability to meet scheduled mail dates this year. Our analysis of our performance to date is disappointing at 8% of all issues mailing either on or before their scheduled date through September. This is compared with our 20% target established for this year. The majority of these delays (approx. 64%) were internal to our Operations Center, while 27% of the delays resulted from receiving material late from the Volunteer Editors. The internal delays are a result of three major challenges we've faced this year.

First, the upgrade of our editing/composition system—our first upgrade in ten years. This upgrade contributed to the delays because of:
—the learning curve for staff in using the new product,
—our move to tag our references more rigorously, to facilitate article linking to our digital library, and

—difficulties in developing the system style sheets to collect individual articles for issue-level printing.

By May 2000, most editing system and style sheet issues were resolved. I am pleased to report that production delays have dropped from a high of 53% down to 0% in September.

Second, the conversion of camera ready copy to a tagged format:
—the process became more labor intensive than anticipated, primarily to provide for quality assurance and consistency of content for our digital library.
—there are surges in volume and problematic electronic graphic files that caused bottlenecks in several areas in our process (e.g., 300 to 500 manuscripts for a single journal issue.)

Third, our most unexpected challenge came from the number of open positions in our editorial staff ranks. Note these snapshots:
—3 open positions and 1 family leave absence in Dec, representing 11% of editorial staff
—3 open positions and 2 family leave absences in Aug, representing 34% of editorial staff.

We're taking a number of actions to improve the editorial staff situation. These include:
—Promoting deserving staff to higher level positions. We are working to more clearly identify career opportunities in journals.
—Filling the gaps in full-time staff with more freelance, part-time and temporary employees.
—Using our production staff rather than editors, whenever possible, to incorporate author revisions to page proofs.
—Outsourcing data entry and processing author proofs to a vendor who has a full complement of our software and is familiar with our composition requirements. Our plan is to develop a second vendor by the end of this year.
—Place a priority on maintaining on-time performance for Volunteer Editors submitting all material on scheduled due dates.

It is important to note that throughout this year we have maintained the high-quality standards for editing and composition. Overall, we are making some good progress and things are improving. We produced 23% of our journals on time in September, compared with 0% on time in April. Volunteer Editors who have been most affected by our delays have been extremely patient. I would like to express my thanks to you as we work to resolve our performance issues. Our editorial staff will continue to communicate with you individually on the status of your issues and I will also keep you informed of our progress on a monthly basis.

Sincerely,

Frank Martinez

Frank Martinez

Staff Director, Publishing Operations

Exhibit 2f. A letter from a manager to volunteers.

2B. Read the dialogue from the film *Cool Hand Luke* in Exhibit 2g. Carr (played by Clifton James) is a prison staff member addressing a new prisoner named Luke (played by Paul Newman). What is Carr's primary organizational goal in this situation? Does Carr primarily inform, direct, consult, or value his audience? Is his message effective?

Carr: Them clothes got laundry numbers on 'em. You . . . always wear the ones that has your number. Any man forgets his number spends the night in the box.. . . There's no playin' grab-ass or fightin' in the buildin'. You got a grudge against another man, you fight him Saturday afternoon. Any man playin' grab-ass or fightin' in the buildin' spends a night in the box. First bell is at five minutes of 8:00, . . . Last bell is at 8:00. Any man not in his bunk at 8:00 spends a night in the box. . . . You'll get two sheets—every Saturday. You put the clean sheet on the top and the top sheet on the bottom and the bottom sheet you turn into the laundry boy. Any man turns in the wrong sheet spends a night in the box. . . . Any man don't bring back his empty pop bottle spends a night in the box. . . . Any man loud-talkin' spends a night in the box. . . . I'm Carr, the floor-walker. I'm responsible for order in here. Any man don't keep order spends a night in . . .
Luke: [interrupting] the box.
Carr: I hope you ain't gonna be a hard case.

Exhibit 2g. Scene from *Cool Hand Luke*.

3

Leader-Member Relationship Quality

Accurately gauging relationship quality is perhaps the greatest obstacle to thinking like a leader. In this chapter, you will learn about the importance of the quality of the relationship between leaders and the members of their organization and, most importantly, how to assess that quality accurately.

Leader-Member Exchange

First proposed by George B. Graen and his colleagues, Leader Member Exchange (LMX) is distinguished from other leadership theories by its focus on the relationship between the leader and the individual members of the organization. According to LMX, the quality of the relationship that develops will predict outcomes at the individual, group, and organizational levels. At the individual level, the more creative members of an organization are likely to have higher quality relationships with their leader, while the least creative are likely to have lower quality relationships.

To explore the group-level outcomes that result from the quality of the relationship between a leader and organizational members, let's consider the case of former New York City Mayor Rudolph Guiliani and his problematic relationship with the African American community. Guiliani had a history of refusing to meet with the individual leaders of that group and of siding with individual law enforcement officers who were accused of unfairly targeting members of that group. Things came to a head when four police officers shot a young, unarmed West African immigrant 41 times in the doorway of his apartment building in the Bronx. Barbara Kellerman describes Guiliani's response to the shooting in her book *Bad Leadership*:

> Guiliani's immediate response to the tragedy was judged to be weak. "It obviously troubles both the Police Commissioner and me that 41 shots were fired," he said. "We don't know the reason for it at this point, but that is what the investigation is all about." There were no heartfelt expressions of sympathy from the mayor, nor much apparent empathy for the large numbers of his constituents who chafed under his leadership, convinced that he considered them second-class citizens. (2005: 121-122)

After Guiliani's response, protests erupted and more than one thousand people were arrested for participating in demonstrations.

For our purposes, it is important to note that the poor quality of Guiliani's relationships with individual African American leaders influenced the response of the entire group of African Americans when they heard his message.

In-groups and Out-groups

LMX recognizes that leaders have different quality relationships with the individual members in their organization. Although that quality is most accurately measured on a continuum from high to medium to low, it has been commonplace to label some members as the "in-group" and others as the "out-group." In-group members have higher quality relationships with the leader than do members in the out-group. In-group members share more information with the leader (as both initiators and receivers); they also have more opportunities to participate in decision-making. In contrast, out-group members have fewer interactions with their leader, and most of those involve formal supervision. In the case of Guiliani, individuals in law enforcement were perceived as in-group members, while African Americans were perceived as out-group members.

To better connect in-groups and out-groups to the communication behavior of leaders, let's reconsider the situation described in the previous chapter in which the leader's primary organizational goals are transactional (maximizing output and consolidating processes).

Leader: Where are we on the system upgrade plan?
Member: We had hoped to finish our analysis last week but we are concerned about potential impacts to the security team. Bill noticed . . .
Leader: [interrupting] Our report has to be ready next week.
Member: I think we need more information before we recommend changes to the system.
Leader: More information won't make this problem easier to solve.

Exhibit 3a. A problematic interaction between leader and member.

If this is the end of the interaction, the quality of the relationship between the leader and member is probably lower after this dialogue. If the member involved is one of the in-group, this single dialogue is not likely to be crucial because there have been and will continue to be others in which the member is able to influence the judgment of his leader. However, if the member involved is one of the out-group, this single dialogue lowers an already low-quality relationship and simply adds more evidence that the leader is uninterested in the member's potential contributions.

Not surprisingly, there are seriously negative implications for members in the out-group: They are likely to experience lower job satisfaction, to receive poorer performance appraisals and lower salaries, and to make less career progress—regardless of their actual performance. Let me repeat: *regardless* of their actual performance.

To make matters worse, research has shown that leaders and members don't agree about the quality of their relationship. Leaders appear to overestimate that quality consistently and sometimes drastically. The TILL system, however, requires that you recognize whether a member is one of your in-group. Because an accurate assessment of relationships is essential, I'll introduce some techniques for measuring their quality in the following section.

Measures of LMX Quality

To obtain the most accurate measure of relationship quality, you might have members use the typical LMX survey instrument reproduced in Figure 3a.

1. How well do you feel that your leader understands your problems and needs?
   (1) not at all (2) somewhat (3) average (4) quite well (5) perfectly

2. How well do you feel that your leader recognizes your potential?
   (1) not at all (2) somewhat (3) average (4) quite well (5) perfectly

3. Regardless of how much formal organizational authority your leader has built into his/her position, what are the chances that he/she would be personally inclined to use power to help you solve problems in your work?
   (1) not inclined (2) somewhat inclined (3) fairly inclined (4) very inclined (5) highly inclined

4. Again, regardless of the amount of formal authority your leader has, to what extent can you count on him/her to "bail you out" at his/her expense when you really need it?
   (1) rarely (2) not often (3) sometimes (4) often (5) almost always

5. How would you characterize your working relationship with your leader?
   (1) very poor (2) poor (3) average (4) good (5) very good

6. I have enough confidence in my leader that I would defend and justify his/her decisions if he/she were not present to do so.
   (1) strongly disagree (2) disagree (3) neutral (4) agree (5) strongly agree

7. Do you usually feel that you know where you stand . . . do you really know how satisfied your leader is with what you do?
   (1) rarely (2) seldom (3) sometimes (4) often (5) almost always

Figure 3a. Member survey for measuring LMX quality.

An average score above 4.0 for these seven questions indicates that the member is one of the in-group. Note that the results of this member survey will be useful to you only if the member feels completely comfortable giving you truthful answers. This is likely only when the results are kept anonymous or are reported to someone other than you. Neither of these conditions, however, will provide you with the information you need about the quality of your relationship with an individual member of your organization.

Because of these limitations of the LMX survey, Figure 3b provides an alternative self-test you can take to assess the quality of your relationship with a member. You must be brutally honest with yourself if the results are to be useful in your goal to think like a leader.

1. List the members you consider excellent employees.
2. Which of the members in your list require little supervision?
3. Which of the members in your list do you like very much as a person?
4. Which of the members in your list would you "bail out"—even at your own expense— if he or she really needed it?

Figure 3b. Leader self-test for measuring relationship quality.

The members you list at least three times in this self-test are in-group members. All others are not (although they may be mid-group rather than out-group members).

The Bottom Line: Thinking Like a Leader

The tools presented in this chapter should help you assess the quality of your relationships with members more accurately. To think like a leader requires that you answer the question: *Is the member one of your in-group?*

It bears repeating that you are likely to overestimate the quality of your relationships with members!

Further Reading

Dainton, M. and Zelley, E. D. (2005) *Applying Communication Theory for Professional Life: A Practical Introduction*. Thousand Oaks, CA: Sage.

This book is a comprehensive textbook on communication theory and its applicability within professional settings. Chapter 6 is on leadership and includes a discussion of LMX. This would be a good starting point for learning more about the ideas in this chapter.

Bass, B. M. (1990). Bass & Stogdill's Handbook of Leadership Theory, Research, & Managerial Applications, 3rd ed. New York: The Free Press.

Dubrin, A. J. (2003). *Leadership: Research Findings, Practice, and Skills*, 4th ed. Boston: Houghton Mifflin.

Hackman, M. Z. & Johnson, C. E. (2003) *Leadership: A Communication Perspective*, 4th ed. Waveland Press.

All three of the books listed above provide comprehensive treatments of leadership, including LMX. Hackman and Johnson's book is noteworthy because of its specific focus on communication in leadership.

Applications

3A. Consider the interaction in Exhibit 3b from the film *Hunt for Red October*. A group of ten Russian naval officers are in the small officer's mess on a nuclear submarine in the Atlantic Ocean. There are many overlapping conversations going on among small groups. Captain Ramius (played by Sean Connery) is seated at the head of a table eating. Executive Officer Borodin (played by Sam Neill) is standing nearby. Borodin and Ramius make eye contact, and Borodin walks toward the ship's doctor, who is putting food on a plate and talking with another officer.

Based on this brief dialogue, which officers would you place in the leader's in-group? Explain based on the behaviors described. Who would you place in the leader's out-group? Why?

Borodin: Excuse me, Doctor. Do you have the figures for the latest batch of radiation tests?

Doctor: [slight pause] Now?

Borodin: [smiling apologetically and nodding] Now. [putting his hand on the doctor's shoulder]

Borodin: Thank you, Doctor [closing and locking the door as he exits]

[all conversations stop, and the remaining men take their seats around the table headed by the captain. Borodin quietly sits next to the captain]

Slavin: [looking at the table in front of him] . . . Captain. I'd like to know exactly what happened to Putin.

Ramius: [completely focused on his food—reaches for salt and continues eating]

Slavin: [looking at the captain] He didn't slip on his tea, did he?

Borodin: I don't think I like your tone, Slavin.

Slavin: What the hell has my tone got to do with it? We're risking our lives here . . . .

Borodin: Look, Putin could have caused complications. [pause] . . . . Did you think that he would just go away and sulk while we carried out our plans? . . .

Captain: [continues looking at his plate of food, cutting meat, and chewing]

Yuri: Are you saying he was murdered? [pause] My God. [looking at the captain] [interchange continues]

Slavin: So he was murdered. . . . The man was a pig. But it's a decision we should have all made together.
Borodin: [with authority] You are not in command here. . . .
[overlapping talk of all officers at the table—except the captain who continues focusing on his food]
Unnamed Officer: We could still go back.
Ramius: [looking up from his meal for the first time] There will be no going back. [pauses to chew and swallow] Before we sailed, I dispatched a letter to Admiral Pedorin in which I announced our intention to defect. . . .
Borodin: [looks at the captain with a shocked expression]

Exhibit 3b. Interaction among a group of Russian naval officers in *Hunt for Red October*.

3B. Consider the dialogue in Exhibit 3c from the film *Ghandi*. Mahatma Ghandi (played by Ben Kingsley) is addressing a large room full of Indian men (both Hindu and Muslim) about a new law designed to quell a nationalist uprising against the British. Who would you place in Ghandi's in-group? Give at least two specific examples from the dialogue to support your answer.

Gandhi: I want to welcome you all. [looking at the three British representatives] Every one of you. . . . Let us begin [with] General Smuts' new law: All Indians must now be fingerprinted, . . . [and only] a Christian marriage is considered valid. Under this Act, our wives and mothers are whores, . . . And our policemen, passing an Indian dwelling . . . may enter and demand the card of any Indian woman whose dwelling it is. [pause] Understand, he does not have to stand at the door. He may enter.
Muslim Audience Member #1: I will not allow it.
Muslim Audience Member #2: . . . I'll kill the man who offers that insult to my home and my wife. . . .
Hindu Audience Member #1: . . . Talk means nothing! Kill a few officials before they disgrace one Indian woman! . . .
Hindu Audience Member #2: In that cause, I would be willing to die!!
Gandhi: I praise such courage. . . . because in this cause I, too, am prepared to die. But, . . . there is no cause for which I am prepared to kill. Whatever they do, we will attack no one, kill no one, . . . They will imprison us, . . . They will seize our possessions, but they cannot take away our self-respect . . .
Hindu Audience Member #3: They beat us and torture us! I say that we should . . .
Gandhi: [interrupting] I am asking you to fight . . . against their anger, not to provoke it. We will not strike a blow, but we will receive them. And through our pain we will make them see their injustice, . . . They may torture my body . . . even kill me. [But], they will have my dead body—not my obedience. . . . Let us take a solemn oath, . . . that come what may we will not submit to this law.

Exhibit 3c. Scene from *Ghandi*.

4

Member Ego Needs and Manager Actions

Praise from, and time with, their manager. That's what employees most want as recognition for the job they do. A survey of 1,500 employees in the banking industry found that three of the top ten items employees most wanted were related to praise from their managers (including hearing "thank you") and number six on that survey was the manager's time (Nelson 2003). In this chapter, you will learn how your actions affect the ego needs of your members. Your ability to predict the effect of your messages on members' ego needs is absolutely critical to thinking like a leader.

Ego Needs

Ego needs refer to a fundamental (and universal) desire to have other people show that they value our personal qualities and social roles. Ego needs are called "positive face wants" within the field of sociolinguistics, referring to the popular idea of "saving face."

Consider an example from the book *The Helmsleys*:

> Leona, on an unexpected inspection tour enters a [hotel] room, spots a crease on a bedspread, a piece of lint on the floor or dresser, a crooked lampshade, anything. She screams imprecations, obscenities: "The maid's a slob. Get her out of here. Out! Out!" (Hammer 1990: 182)

Although examples of famous individuals are perhaps more entertaining, I have collected numerous examples of less famous managers threatening the ego needs of members. Consider the anonymous narrative below from an organizational member about an interaction with a manager.

> *I came in at least 20 minutes early every morning. One morning I came at 8:05 and the "bitch" just started in about being late. She was all over me about being to work on time, and I just ate it up. It pissed me off to no end that it didn't matter about how early I came in, but it did matter when I came in late. So, I just kept coming in late.*

When managers threaten the personal value of members by focusing on what they do wrong and ignoring what they do right, those members respond with anger, perceptions of injustice, and retaliation.

In the case of Leona Helmsley and the anonymous manager, their behavior undermined rather than built organizational commitment as shown in the COMPETING VALUES FRAMEWORK (Figure 2a). In short, they did not lead.

Let's compare the following narrative, to the preceding one.

> *One time in particular, [my boss] approached me to tell me that I was doing a really great job and that everyone had been bragging on my hard work. She proceeded to tell me "thank you" for the hard work I had been giving towards the office. It made me feel really important to know that she was paying attention to the small people in the office where about 50 are employed.*

In this situation, the manager did act as a leader by attending to the ego needs of the member and building commitment to the organization.

One way managers signal the value they place on members is by spending time with them. Helen Spencer-Oatey says this specialized type of ego need is related to "the type and extent of our involvement with others" and "the extent to which we share concerns, feelings and interests" (2000: 15). The following example was written by an anonymous employee.

> *I'm responsible for selling advertising. One of my accounts had failed to sign an annual contract. The advertising director (my direct supervisor) had indicated that he would handle the problem with the account. Several weeks passed and he didn't contact the account. I gave him a note reminding him that I didn't have a contract. He came to my desk and threw the note on my desk and said he didn't have to be reminded that he would handle it when he got ready.*

The manager in this situation threatened the ego needs of the employee when he did not follow through or even explain why he had not yet contacted the sales representative's customer. Clearly, the manager made a bad situation worse with his reaction to the employee's request, whereby the employee was attempting to get his ego needs met. The manager's behavior undermined rather than improved organizational commitment as shown in the COMPETING VALUES FRAMEWORK (Figure 2a) because he made the member feel excluded rather than included. He clearly did not function as a leader.

Contrast the previous example, with the following one.

> *My new boss is amazing. She is always willing to help me whenever I need her. Because this is new to me, she is extremely patient and always answers any question I ask.*

In this situation, the manager tended the employee's need for time with the leader by making herself available for questions.

Manager Actions

Whether managers are acting as entrepreneurs, mediators, resource allocators, or negotiators, their decisions show what value they place on organizational members' ego needs. Managers tend to members' ego needs (and build organizational commitment) by making decisions that demonstrate the members' value to the organization and that include members in conversation, meetings, etc. Conversely, managers threaten members' ego needs when they exclude them from those interactions by ignoring or even interrupting them. For instance, imagine a situation in which a female manager and an organizational member (a male engineer) have the conversation in Exhibit 4a.

Leader: Where are we on the system upgrade plan?
Member: We had hoped to finish our analysis last week but we are concerned about potential impacts to the security team. Bill noticed . . .
Leader: [interrupting] Our report has to be ready next week.
Member: I think we need more information before we recommend changes to the system.
Leader: How much time are you thinking you'll need? [facing member and making eye contact]

Exhibit 4a. Positive effect of a leader's message on the ego needs of a member.

The manager's final response will have a much more positive effect on the engineer's ego needs than the response in the following version of the same conversation.

Leader: Where are we on the system upgrade plan?
Member: We had hoped to finish our analysis last week but we are concerned about potential impacts to the security team. Bill noticed . . .
Leader: [interrupting] Our report has to be ready next week.
Member: I think we need more information before we recommend changes to the system.
Leader: Look, more information won't make this problem easier to solve. [walking away]

Exhibit 4b. Negative effect of a leader's message on the ego needs of a member.

In Exhibit 4a, the manager's final response is a question that clearly communicates that she values the opinion of the engineer and that she is willing to take time to adjust her plans in order to consider his suggestion. However, in Exhibit 4b, the manager's final response clearly communicates that she does not value the engineer's opinion—she discounts or attempts to dismiss it by disagreeing with his suggestion that more information is needed and ends their interaction by walking away. (Note the absence of "leave taking," such as *Bye, See ya later*, etc.) In 4b, the leader's primary organizational goal (maximizing output) drives her to act by informing the member that she disagrees with his suggestion (lower left quadrant of Figure 2a).

Unfortunately, managers often have to deal with subjects that have potential negative effects on the ego needs of members. At times, managers must reprimand members or raise emotional topics like poor performance because of their mandate to focus on organizational tasks or goals. As decision makers, managers must determine which members should share in the decision-making process and how much weight their opinions should be afforded. In the role of informational nerve center, managers must choose the members with whom they share information, as well as how much information to share. Effective leaders, however, are able to focus on relationships and tasks simultaneously—at least much of the time. (Think back to Chapter 1 to Hunter's conversation with the seaman in *Crimson Tide*.)

Consider yet another version of the conversation between the female manager and male engineer in Exhibit 4c.

Leader: Where are we on the system upgrade plan?
Member: We had hoped to finish our analysis last week but we are concerned about potential impacts to the security team. Bill noticed . . .
Leader: [interrupting] Our report has to be ready next week.
Member: I think we need more information before we recommend changes to the system.
Leader: I rely on you because I know you want to make the best decision possible. But we can't delay to collect more information in this case because the costs are too high.

Exhibit 4c. Mitigating the negative effect of a leader's message on the ego needs of a member.

In Exhibit 4c, the manager's primary organizational goal (maximizing output) drives her to act by informing the member that she disagrees with his suggestion (lower left quadrant of Figure 2a), but she also communicates the value she places on the member's contributions (upper left quadrant of Figure 2a) in order to mitigate the negative effect of that disagreement.

Before we move on, I need to make two points. First, both leaders and members have ego needs. It is important to distinguish between affecting others' ego needs (e.g., when you compliment or criticize a member's idea) and affecting your own ego needs (e.g., when you compliment or criticize your own idea). In Exhibit 4d we have a sample email sent from an IT manager to her "customers" within her organization. Many of us receive messages like this one from the people who manage our email systems. Note that the first few paragraphs provide information to organizational members about the cause of their email problems, and the final sentence is an apology for those problems. I believe the writer placed the apology last and devoted little space to it in order to protect her own ego. Her concern was not for the members receiving her message.

From: Jan V. Crumb
Sent: Wednesday, January 23, 2005 9:46 AM
To: Staff
Subject: Yesterday's EMAIL server outage

Yesterday afternoon, the Exchange Server (the system that provides you email) shut itself down.

The system never reported an error or gave any other indication as to why it failed. We did however observe that the virus scanning software was dealing with an exceptional number of incoming e-mail messages that contained viruses.

The virus scanning software attempts to clean or otherwise remove the contaminated portion of the message. The best guess at the moment is the system was overwhelmed by the number.

We continue to look for the best products on the market to handle this problem.

We regret the inconvenience such disruptions cause and will continue to work to minimize all service disruptions.

Thanks,
+~+~+~+~+~+~+~+~+~+~+~+~+~+~+
Jan V. Crumb
Director of Technology
Yahoo State University
Yahoo, AL 55555
Phone: 205-555-1212
FAX: 205-555-2222

Exhibit 4d. A manager focusing on her own ego needs.

The important point here is that, when leaders are unwilling or hesitant to apologize or confess, they are motivated by their desire not to threaten ego needs—but it is their own ego, not the member's, that is at stake. This kind of attention to ego needs is not good leadership. Rather, it is your ability to predict the effect of your message on your *member's* ego that is crucial to your success in thinking like a leader.

The second point I want to make is that ego needs are both individual (as in Exhibit 4c) and group-related. When you compliment or criticize a group to which members belong (e.g., women, Southerners, IT employees, etc.), their ego needs are affected. Think back to our discussion in Chapter 3 of Rudy Guiliani and his tepid response to the police shooting in the Bronx. He clearly threatened the ego needs of the entire African American community, judging by the magnitude of the ensuing demonstrations. Everyone has group-related ego needs, but they are crucially important in collectivist cultures (e.g., Guatemala, Hong Kong, Saudi Arabia, Japan, etc.). I'll discuss the role of culture in individual members' needs in the following chapter.

The Bottom Line: Thinking Like a Leader

This chapter introduced you to the concept of ego needs and described how managers commonly affect the ego needs of organizational members. To think like a leader requires that you answer the question: *How will my message affect the member's ego needs?*

Answering this question will require that you understand both the individual and group-related ego needs of the member in a specific management situation.

Further Reading

Dainton, M. and Zelley, E. D. (2005) *Applying Communication Theory for Professional Life: A Practical Introduction*. Thousand Oaks, CA: Sage.

This book is an appropriate starting point for further explorations of the concept of ego needs as it is a textbook aimed at advanced undergraduates or graduate students. Chapter 3 on interpersonal communication includes a section on "politeness" which includes the concept of ego or "face."

Brown, P. and Levinson, S. C. (1987) *Politeness: Some Universals in Language Usage*. (Studies in Interactional Sociolinguistics, vol. 4). Cambridge: Cambridge University Press.

Goffman, E. (1967) *Interaction Ritual: Essays on Face to Face Behavior*. New York: Pantheon Books.

Spencer-Oatey, H. (2000) *Culturally Speaking: Managing Rapport Through Talk Across Cultures*. London: Continuum Press.

All three of these books are highly academic. However, they are the primary theoretical works upon which much of the TILL system is based. All use the term "face" rather than "ego."

Applications

4A. To practice recognizing and categorizing the ego needs involved in interactions, read the dialogue below from the film *Working Girl*. The interaction is between two managers, Mr. Turkel (played by James Lally) and Mr. Lutz (played by Oliver Platt) and their direct report, Tess McGill (played by Melanie Griffith). Tess has applied to the "Entre Program," the management trainee program within their organization. What is the primary organizational goal driving the two managers to communicate with Tess in this situation? Whose ego needs are tended to or threatened in this situation? Explain using specific examples.

Mr. Turkel: . . . Tess, I have some good news and some bad news. . . . they turned you down for the Entre Program again.
Tess: Why?
Mr. Lutz: We did all we could, Tessy.
Mr. Turkel: I mean, you have to remember, you're up against Harvard and Wharton graduates. What do you got? Some night school, some secretarial time on your sheet?
Mr. Lutz: Christians and lions, Tess. . . .
Tess: And the good news? . . .
Mr. Lutz: Bob in Arbitrage. You're so hungry. They're looking for hungry down there!
Tess: Really?
Mr. Lutz: . . . Bob's looking for a new assistant and wants to meet you for a drink.
Tess: This isn't another set-up?
Mr. Lutz: Do I look like a pimp? Bob says he's looking for hungry, I think to myself, "Tess." . . .
Tess: Bob in Arbitrage.
Mr. Lutz: Bob Speck. Extension 256. He's expecting your call. Go get 'em, Tessy!

Exhibit 4e. Scene from *Working Girl*.

4B. Read the scene described in Exhibit 4f from the film *The Patriot*. The interaction takes place as the representatives of the colony of South Carolina (including Benjamin Martin, played by Mel Gibson) are asked by Colonel Harry Burwell (played by Chris Cooper) to join eight other colonies who have levied a tax to support a war of independence against Great Britain. What is the primary organizational goal driving Colonel Burwell in this situation? Are

Benjamin Martin's ego needs tended or threatened in this situation? Explain using specific examples from the dialogue.

Colonel Burwell: This is not a war for the independence of one or two colonies, but . . . of one nation.
[Several representatives speak]
Benjamin Martin: Why should I trade one tyrant three thousand miles away for three thousand tyrants one mile away? An elected legislature can trample a man's rights as easily as a King can.
Colonel Burwell: Captain Martin, I understood you to be a patriot.
Benjamin Martin: If you mean by "patriot," am I angry about taxation without representation? Yes, I am. . . . But . . . am I willing to go to war with England? . . . the answer is most definitely no!
Middleton: This from the same Captain . . . Martin whose fury was so famous during the Wilderness Campaign. [Middleton continues to deride Martin] . . .
Colonel Burwell: Mister Middleton, I fought with Captain Martin under Washington . . . . There is not a man in this room, or anywhere, for that matter, to whom I would more willingly trust my life. . . . [addresses Martin] Benjamin, I was at Bunker Hill. The British advanced three times and we killed over seven hundred of them at point blank range, and still they took the ground. That is the measure of their resolve. Now, if your principles dictate independence, then war is the only way. It has come to that.
Benjamin Martin: . . . My wife is dead. Now who's to care for [my seven children] if I go to war?
Colonel Burwell: Wars are not fought only by childless men.
Benjamin Martin: Granted. But . . . the innocent will die with the rest of us. I will not fight. And . . . I will not cast a vote that will send others to fight in my stead.
Colonel Burwell: And your principles?
Benjamin Martin: I'm a parent. I haven't got the luxury of principles.

Exhibit 4f. Scene from *The Patriot*.

5
Member Autonomy Needs and Manager Actions

In the survey of 1,500 employees in the banking industry mentioned in the previous chapter, autonomy and authority ranked as the fourth and fifth most important items employees desire as recognition for the job they do (Nelson 2003). In this chapter, you will learn how your actions can affect the autonomy needs of your members. Once again, your ability to predict the effect of your messages on your members is absolutely crucial to thinking like a leader.

Autonomy Needs

Autonomy needs refer to a fundamental (and universal) desire to have other people acknowledge our right to freedom of action. Autonomy needs are often called "negative face wants" within sociolinguistics. Consider an example from an anonymous employee:

> *Once my boss called me on a Sunday afternoon. He asked me to come work for a few hours. To me, Sundays are for relaxation. I had no plans for the afternoon and I was just relaxing in shorts and a t-shirt. He called without any prior notice and asked me to come to work. I can't really say "no" to the boss because then I'm afraid he would hold it against me. I was really frustrated and mad because he had complete control over my day at that point.*

The manager in this situation threatened the autonomy needs of the employee by redirecting the employee's actions. Such threats often result in perceptions of injustice in the workplace. The manager's communication behavior undermined rather than built organizational commitment as shown in the COMPETING VALUES FRAMEWORK (Figure 2a). This is not a positive example of leadership.

Compare the following narrative from another anonymous employee.

> *The first day on my job I rode with a fellow employee to learn how to perform my duties. What impressed me about the supervisor was how much responsibility he gave me on my second day of the job. He gave me a list of places that needed supplies and informed me that he trusted my judgment and said that I can make my own routes as long as I made at least five drop-offs per day. His giving me this flexibility gave me the incentive to*

work really hard, because I felt like I had a very important job that I was solely responsible for. By the end of the summer I was making around ten to twelve stops per day and they gave me an award for my hard work. I believe [the boss] giving me my own choices made me a more productive worker and helped me feel more part of the team.

In this situation, the leader tended to the member's need for autonomy by giving the member the freedom to decide how do the job. In this situation, the manager did act as a leader by building trust with the employee.

Manager Actions

As we saw in Chapter 4, managers' roles often place them in situations with the potential to affect the ego needs of members. The same is true for autonomy rights. Managers' decisions show the extent to which they trust their members to perform without supervision (i.e., their autonomy needs). Managers tend to members' autonomy needs (and build organizational commitment) by making decisions that allow the members ownership of their work. Managers threaten members' autonomy needs every time they micromanage their members' work.

Let's return to the situation in which a female leader and an organizational member (a male engineer) have the following conversation:

Leader: Where are we on the system upgrade plan?
Member: We had hoped to finish our analysis last week but we are concerned about potential impacts to the security team. Bill noticed . . .
Leader: [interrupting] Our report has to be ready next week.
Member: I think we need more information before we recommend changes to the system
Leader: I know Ann is the obvious person to gather that information, but I can't spare her right now. I'll give you until the 8th to dig around if you think it will help.

Exhibit 5a. Positive effect of a leader's message on the autonomy needs of a member.

Remember that the leader's primary organizational goal (maximizing output) drives her to act by informing the member that she disagrees with his suggestion. Her final response in Exhibit 5a will have a much more positive effect on the engineer's autonomy needs than the response in the alternate version of the same conversation in Exhibit 5b.

Leader: Where are we on the system upgrade plan?
Member: We had hoped to finish our analysis last week but we are concerned about potential impacts to the security team. Bill noticed . . .
Leader: [interrupting] Our report has to be ready next week.
Member: I think we need more information before we recommend changes to the system.
Leader: I'll give you until the 8th to dig around if you think it will help.

Exhibit 5b. Negative effect of a leader's message on the autonomy needs of a member.

In Exhibit 5b, the manager may be threatening the member's autonomy rights (his right not to be imposed upon unfairly) if the member feels it is someone else's responsibility to get more information. However, the manager's final response in Exhibit 5a communicates that she values the autonomy of the member by recognizing the imposition associated with him collecting more information. Thus, the intrinsic threat is mitigated in Exhibit 5a because the leader acts not only by informing the member of her disagreement but also by demonstrating that she values his autonomy (upper left quadrant of Figure 2a).

Unfortunately, because of their decision-making role, managers must often act in ways that threaten the autonomy needs of members. For example, managers must assign or remind members about tasks, make requests or suggestions, offer advice, and give warnings because of their mandate to focus on organizational goals. As I've stated before, effective leaders are able to focus on relationships and tasks simultaneously—at least most of the time.

Differences Among Members

Before we move on, I need to discuss the potential influence of individual and cultural differences on the needs of organizational members. Although such differences can influence both ego and autonomy needs, I will focus on autonomy needs because understanding that will go a long way toward helping you think like a leader. We'll briefly consider three issues: (1) the readiness of individual members, (2) the values of individual members and their native cultures, and (3) the choice of media for communicating with members.

Readiness of a Member

Let's go back to the second anonymous narrative at the beginning of this chapter (the one involving an employee who was granted considerable autonomy on the second day of work). As this narrative was being discussed, you may have thought that giving such autonomy to a different employee could have been a disaster. And you would be right.

Much leadership research recognizes that leaders must adapt their behavior toward members according to each member's individual needs. For our purposes, one useful way of categorizing such needs comes from the Hersey-Blanchard Tri-dimensional Leadership Model (Hersey & Blanchard 1988). In any situation involving a member performing a task, the member's need for autonomy (i.e., "readiness") will be highest when the member is both able and willing to perform that task. The member's ability is dictated by his or her knowledge, experience, and skill vis-à-vis the specific task. The member's willingness is dictated by his or her confidence, commitment, and motivation vis-à-vis the specific task. In situations involving members whose ability or willingness to perform a specific task is low, their need for autonomy is lower than their their ego needs (e.g., their need for help from their manager).

To illustrate, read the email in Exhibit 5c written by the leader of a work team comprised of 13 volunteers within a non-profit organization; the goal of the team was to develop plans to involve citizens in local activities.

> From: Maria Fuentes
> Sent: Thursday, March 20, 2005 4:57 PM
> To: Volunteer Staff
> Subject: Update on our plan
>
> When you have recorded the key points as answers to the above questions, write the paragraph that expresses the essence/rationale of why this is the best approach. Do it from the point of view of its proponents emphasizing what is seen as most valuable about the choice.

Exhibit 5c. Memo privileging members' autonomy needs over their ego needs.

Because 8 of the 13 volunteers who received this email felt both capable and willing to complete the task specified by the leader, her message was effective for them. However, for the other five volunteers, her message was ineffective because they needed more of her time and attention in order to understand how to complete the task. The leader met the needs of the first group of volunteers: They had high autonomy and low ego needs. But she did not meet the low autonomy and high ego needs of the second group.

Values of a Member

Another way in which leaders must adapt their behavior toward an individual member relates to the values of that member. Such ethnic, religious, and social values are acquired from the member's culture. Geert Hofstede's (2001) study of 100,000 IBM employees in more than 50 nations provides a clear method

for classifying cultural values (although his classification has been the subject of debate). Let's consider just two of Hofstede's four dimensions.
The first dimension, "power distance," describes the relative equality of members within a culture. If we consider only power distance, Mexico, for example, has a highly centralized and authoritarian power structure, producing members who expect leaders to take charge. The U.S., in contrast, has a democratic power structure with members who expect to participate in decision-making with leaders. The second dimension, "uncertainty avoidance," describes the relative comfort level with unpredictable and unstructured situations. Japan, for example (with its low tolerance for uncertainty) has a high uncertainty avoidance culture in which members want clear rules and view age and experience as highly desirable. The U.S., however (with its greater tolerance for uncertainty) has a low uncertainty avoidance culture, producing members who take risks and view their own intuition as trustworthy.

Clearly these two dimensions have implications for autonomy needs. When you are first developing a relationship with a member from Mexico, you might provide less autonomy than you would for new members in general. Likewise, in the early stages of a relationship with a member from Japan, you might give more detailed directions about your expectations for a project than you would for other new members. To further illustrate, read the dialogue in Exhibit 5d between a leader from the U.S. and his Greek subordinate, whose native culture has relatively high "power distance" and low "uncertainty avoidance."

Leader: How long will it take you to finish this report?
Member: I do not know. How long should it take?
Leader: You are in the best position to analyze time requirements.
Member: Ten days.
Leader: Take fifteen. Is it agreed you will do it in fifteen days?

Exhibit 5d. Interchange between participants from cultures with different "power differences." (Adapted from Hackman & Johnson 2004:306)

Unfortunately, in this situation, the leader's attempt to tend to the autonomy needs of the member by allowing him to set his own deadline failed miserably. When the member was unable to meet his own unrealistic deadline—even after working night and day for 15 days—he handed in his resignation, believing that his boss was at fault for not knowing how much time the task should have required. He didn't want to work for someone who was "incompetent." In this case, the member, who was from a high power distance culture, expected the leader to take charge. The leader, who comes from a low power distance culture, shoved the burden for decision-making back on the employee.

Such value differences also exist between subgroups within a culture. In Deborah Tannen's study of male and female bosses in the U.S., she writes,

> American men are likely to place relatively greater value on independence, whereas American women are likely to place more relative value on involvement. But I wonder if it is right to see "autonomy-invested" as opposed to "people-oriented." It seems . . . that [the men] feel giving their subordinates freedom is best for them, personally, as well as for the company, so they are being person-oriented in a different way. (Tannen 1994:188)

In our terms we could say that female leaders generally tend autonomy needs less and ego needs more than male leaders in the U.S. Such tendencies may need to be altered to meet the needs of individual members.

Media Choice

The individualized nature of autonomy needs among members is one reason your choice of medium for interacting with them is so important. The leader's choice to send the email in Exhibit 5c is crucial in determining the effect of her message on the needs of her members. Different media for communicating can be characterized along a continuum of "richness," describing their ability to carry nonverbal cues, convey personality traits, provide rapid feedback, and support the use of natural language (Daft & Lengel 1986). As a "rich" medium, face-to-face interaction is considered personal because it can provide:

- A host of body language (e.g., eye contact) and voice quality (e.g., loudness) cues, which helps us know more about the other interactants' personalities
- Immediate responses to those other interactants
- Natural context (i.e., humans learn to talk face-to-face)

Because rich media require more time spent with others, they are more personal and tend ego needs.

In contrast, as a "lean medium," memos are considered efficient because they provide:

- No body language and few (e.g., all capital letters), if any, voice quality cues, which gives us little information about personality
- Delayed responses to or from other interactants (i.e., the writer initiates interaction when the reader is not present)

- Unnatural context (i.e., humans learn to write memos only after mastering richer media)

Because lean media require less time spent with others, they are more efficient and tend autonomy needs. Figure 5a illustrates the relative "richness" of four common media for communicating in the contemporary business world. One of the reasons email has become so widespread may be that it has the advantages of both rich media (e.g., there is the potential for more personality cues and more rapid feedback than with a memo) and lean media (e.g., there is also the potential for fewer personality cues and less rapid feedback than on the telephone).

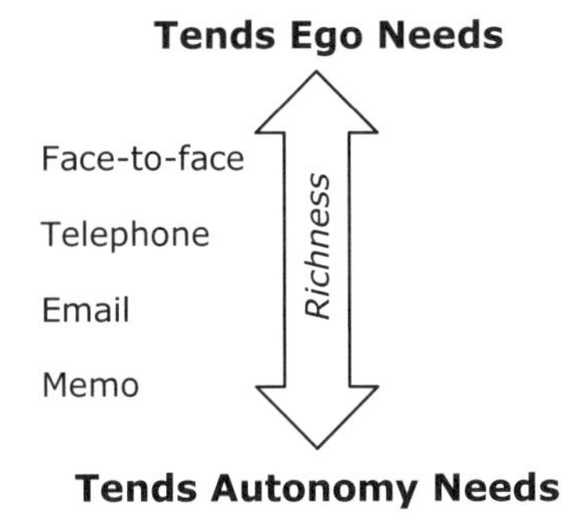

Figure 5a. Different communication media tend different needs.

Because email provides less chance for the audience to provide feedback than a face-to-face meeting, the leader's choice in 5c was problematic for the 5 volunteers who were not ready to complete the task given to them. Those volunteers required a "richer" medium which supported their ego needs. On the other hand, the 8 volunteers who had high autonomy needs were perfectly happy with the leader's choice of email.

Once again, your ability to predict the effect of your messages on each member's autonomy needs is crucial to your success in thinking like a leader.

The Bottom Line: Thinking Like a Leader

This chapter introduced you to the concept of autonomy needs and described how managers commonly affect the autonomy needs of organizational members. To think like a leader requires that you answer the question: *How will your message affect the member's need for autonomy?*

Answering this question will require that you understand the needs of the member based on his or her values and readiness in this specific management situation.

Further Reading

Dainton, M. and Zelley, E. D. (2005) *Applying Communication Theory for Professional Life: A Practical Introduction*. Thousand Oaks, CA: Sage.

This book is an appropriate starting point for further exploration of the concept of autonomy needs as it is a textbook aimed at advanced undergraduates or graduate students. Chapter 3 on interpersonal communication includes a section on "politeness" which includes the concept of autonomy or "negative face."

Hackman, M. Z. & Johnson, C. E. (2003) *Leadership: A Communication Perspective*, 4th ed. Waveland Press.

Hofstede, G. (2004) *Cultures and Organizations: Software of the Mind*, 2nd ed. New York: MacGraw-Hill.

Both books provide an introduction to cultural classification for the layperson. Hackman and Johnson cover this material in Chapter 10 on diversity (pp. 296-307) with specific applications for leaders.

Brown, P. and Levinson, S. C. (1987) *Politeness: Some Universals in Language Usage*. (Studies in Interactional Sociolinguistics, vol. 4). Cambridge: Cambridge University press.

Spencer-Oatey, H. (2000) *Culturally Speaking: Managing Rapport Through Talk Across Cultures*. London: Continuum Press.

Both of these books are highly academic. However, they are the primary theoretical works upon which much of the TILL system is based. Brown and Levinson use the term "negative face wants," and Spencer-Oatey uses the term "equity rights" rather than "autonomy needs."

Applications

5A. To practice recognizing and categorizing the autonomy needs involved in leader-member interactions, consider the dialogue from *Courage Under Fire* in Exhibit 5e. The interaction is between a U.S. Army General (played by Michael Moriarty) and Colonel (played by Denzel Washington) who works for the general and is investigating the actions of Captain Walden (played by Meg Ryan) who died during the Gulf War. The general is under pressure to award the first Medal of Honor to a female military leader. The colonel wants to delay his recommendation because he has received different accounts of the captain's behavior from her subordinates. Their dialogue occurs on a golf course with one of the general's subordinates nearby—within hearing distance. The general is out of uniform since he's playing golf, but the colonel is on duty and interrupts the general's game. What is the primary organizational goal driving the leader in this interaction? Are the member's autonomy needs tended to or threatened in this situation? Explain using specific examples from the dialogue. Are the colonel's readiness and values or the general's choice of medium important in determining the effectiveness of the general's message?

General: Submit your report today. [walking toward his ball]
Colonel: Sorry, Sir. I won't [sign] an incomplete report.
General: [taking a practice swing] Should I remind you who recommended you for this post when no one else would touch you?
Colonel: . . . Are you saying you chose me because I wouldn't rock the boat?
General: Dereliction of duty. . . drunk and disorderly. . . . at best dishonorable discharge, . . . I could give you direct orders to submit your report. . . . I handed this to you, Nat—as a way back. You could have had one helluva career. You give Meredith [the colonel's wife] my best. Tell her I didn't have any choice.
Colonel: I'm gonna finish this report—on my own if I have to. I'm gonna get this one right. [walking away]

Exhibit 5e. Scene from *Courage Under Fire*.

5B. Read the scene in Exhibit 5f from the film, *Office Space*. In this scene, the manager at a software company, Bill Lumbergh (played by Gary Cole), approaches the cubicle of software engineer, Peter Gibbons (played by Ron Livingston). Then read the scene from the same film in Exhibit 5g. In this scene, the interaction takes place between Stan, the manager of a restaurant modeled after TGIFriday's (played by Mike Judge in the movie) and one of the restaurant's waitresses, Joanna (played by Jennifer Anniston). Stan refers to the number of pins or buttons (called "flair" by the restaurant management) that Joanna is wearing on her uniform.

Compare the primary organizational goal driving each manager to communicate with his subordinate in these two situations. How are the members' autonomy needs affected in each situation? Use specific examples from the dialogue to support your answer. Are the members' readiness and values important in determining the effectiveness of the management message? How about each manager's choice of medium?

Lumbergh: Hello, Peter. Uh what's happening? [no pause] Uh we have sort of a problem here. Yeah. You apparently didn't put one of the new cover sheets on your TPS report.
Gibbons : Oh yeah. I'm sorry . . . . I forgot.
Lumbergh: Um yeah. . . . We're putting the cover sheets on all TPS reports now before they go out. Did you see the memo about this?
Gibbons: . . . . Yeah, I have it right here. I just uh forgot. But uh it's not shipping out until tomorrow. So there's no problem.
Lumbergh: Yeah. If you could just go ahead and make sure you do that from now on, that would be great. And uh I'll make sure you get another copy of that memo. OK? [walking away]
Gibbons: I have the memo . . . .

Exhibit 5f. Scene from *Office Space*.

[Stan calls Joanna over as she enters the restaurant to start her shift. Joanna begins to apologize for being late, when Stan interrupts.]
Stan: We need to talk about your flair.
Joanna: I have 15 pieces on.
Stan: Well, 15 is the minimum. . . . It's up to you if you want to do just the bare minimum. Or . . . Bryan, for example, has on 37 pieces.
Joanna: So you want me to wear more.
Stan: . . . People come to Chotchkies for atmosphere and attitude. OK? That's what the flair it about. . . . .
Joanna: [sarcastically] So . . . MORE huh?
Stan: Look, we want you to express yourself. OK? . . . if you feel the bare minimum is enough. Then OK. . . .
Joanna: You know what, Stan, if you want me to wear 37 pieces of flair, like . . . Bryan, why don't you make the minimum 37 pieces . . . ?
Stan: Well, I thought I remembered you saying that you wanted to express yourself.
Joanna: You know what? I DO [but] I don't need 37 pieces of flair to do it. [flips off Stan]

Exhibit 5g. Another scene from *Office Space*.

6
Thinking Like a Leader

To think like a leader requires that you focus on the following questions in any management situation where you intend to interact with one of your members.

1. *What is the organizational purpose driving you to communicate with the member—and how urgent is your need to act?* Chapter 2 provided a framework for categorizing the four organizational goals and intended actions of leaders:

- Leaders INFORM members to consolidate internal organizational processes.
- Leaders DIRECT members to maximize organizational output.
- Leaders CONSULT members to adapt the organization to change.
- Leaders VALUE members to build human commitment and organizational trust.

You must also know how urgent your intended action is within the current situation.

2. *Is the member one of your in-group?* Chapter 3 gave you two techniques for assessing the quality of your relationships with members: One is a short questionnaire to be administered to members working under a leader, and the other is a short self-test a leader can complete to estimate LMX quality among members. I also advised that an inaccurate assessment is often the greatest obstacle to thinking like a leader.

3. *How will your message affect the member's ego needs?* Chapter 4 introduced two types of ego needs:

- The desire to have other people show that they value our personal qualities and social roles.
- The desire to be included by others.

Leaders can tend or threaten the ego needs of members in their organization.

4. *How will your message affect the member's autonomy needs?* Chapter 5 introduced the notion of autonomy—the need for individual freedom.

When you have accurately answered these questions, you know the purpose for your intended interaction with a member, its urgency, and your current relationship with that member, along with the potential effect of your action on your future relationship with that member. In other words, you have assessed the management situation using your emotional intelligence.

At this point, you may be thinking about how incredibly time-consuming it would be to use the TILL heuristic every time you think about interacting with a member. And you would be right. Changing behavior takes self-awareness and self-discipline.

However, don't lose sight of the ultimate importance of improving your leadership communication skills. We know leaders must be expert communicators in order to build better relationships with members and to positively influence productivity, job satisfaction and performance, and organizational effectiveness—but they rarely are.

Applications

6A. Read the annual employee performance evaluation for Doris Johnson, who works as a clerk in the marketing department of a large organization. At the time of the evaluation, she had been employed by the organization for 8 years and 1 month and had served in her current position for 5 years. The evaluation was prepared by Doris' immediate supervisor, Kevin Russell.

Your task is to assess whether Mr. Russell was thinking like a leader when he prepared the evaluation. First, assess the underlying organizational purpose and Mr. Russell's actions performed in this document. (You should assume that Doris does not feel a part of Mr. Russell's in-group before receiving this document.) Second, assess how the document is likely to affect Doris' ego and autonomy needs. Third, predict the effect of this evaluation on the relationship between Doris and Mr. Russell. Point to specific examples in the document to support your assessment.

PART I - PERFORMANCE FACTORS

Knowledge, Skills, Abilities – Consider the degree to which the employee exhibits the required level of job knowledge and/or skills to perform the job and this employee's use of established techniques, materials and equipment as they relate to performance.

Unacceptable Superior

☐ 1 ☐ 2 ☒ 3 ☐ 4 ☐ 5

Comments: You have a thorough fundamental knowledge of the guidelines for doing your job. A site visit to Organization Y revealed a great deal of information we were not familiar with. Effort must be made in the verification and filing responsibilities to proactively prevent tremendous backlogs making it difficult to stay current.

Quality of Work – Does the employee complete assignments meeting quality standards? Consider accuracy, neatness, thoroughness and adherence to standards and safety rules.

Unacceptable Superior

☐ 1 ☒ 2 ☐ 3 ☐ 4 ☐ 5

Comments: We consistently maintain a backlog of incomplete Form 3s, which indicates we are out of compliance with regulations. This was noted on last year's evaluation with an expectation for improvement. The identification of additional requirements that we were not adhering to have caused a backlog due to the scrutiny needed in the verification process. Implementation of these restrictions have been untimely. Current status of compliance with guidelines is difficult to monitor.

Quantity of Work – Consider the results of this employee's efforts. Does the employee demonstrate the ability to manage several responsibilities simultaneously; perform work in a productive and timely manner; meet work schedules?

Unacceptable Superior

☐ 1 ☒ 2 ☐ 3 ☐ 4 ☐ 5

Comments: There is a large volume of work to be processed in your area. I have consistently encouraged you to identify ideas on changing the process to make it attainable. We consistently maintain a backlog of unprocessed or incomplete documents. You must find ways to streamline and accomplish your duties complying with regulations and deadlines.

Work Habits – To what extent does the employee display a positive, cooperative attitude toward work assignments and requirements? Consider compliance with established work rules and organizational policies.

Unacceptable Superior

☐ 1 ☐ 2 ☒ 3 ☐ 4 ☐ 5

Comments: Although your job duties are mostly repetitive, routing processing functions, I can depend on you to report to work and contribute. You uphold the rules we have set for your Area such as requiring individuals to "check out" files and ensure that they are returned. Do not take a defensive stance when constructive criticism is given or your work is evaluated.

Communication – Consider job related effectiveness in dealing with others. Does the employee express ideas clearly both orally and in writing, listen well and respond appropriately?

Unacceptable Superior

☐ 1 ☒ 2 ☐ 3 ☐ 4 ☐ 5

Comments: I continue to receive a lack of information from you regarding the status of the filing, Form 3s, etc. You do not offer to me suggestions or recommendations for improvement to accomplish your work load. You rarely communicate with me unless I initiate email, meeting or conversation. If you do not bring to my attention that things are problematic, I have no way of knowing until I request the information. This allows issues to progress to an unmanageable situation before I am made aware.

PART II - BEHAVIORAL TRAITS

Dependability – Consider the amount of time spent directing this employee. Does the employee monitor projects and exercise follow-through; adhere to time frames; is on time for meetings and appointments; and responds appropriately to instructions and procedures?

Unacceptable Superior

☐ 1 ☒ 2 ☐ 3 ☐ 4 ☐ 5

Comments: The status of the verification of Form 3s and employment eligibility do not adhere to regulations. We have continued to lag in the updating of Form 3s, possibly allowing employment of ineligible individuals. We consistently keep a backlog of file room projects and incomplete Form 3s. You often do not communicate with me the status of these matters until I inquire. Although I do not spend a great deal of time providing supervision to you, the work is not getting accomplished satisfactorily. I do not feel your May 11 response to my instruction was handled in an appropriate manner.

Cooperation – How well does the employee work with co-workers and supervisors as a contributing team member? Does the employee demonstrate consideration of others; maintain rapport with others; help others willingly?

Unacceptable Superior

☐ 1 ☐ 2 ☒ 3 ☐ 4 ☐ 5

Comments: You seem to work well with co-workers and those who complete the Form 3s in the field. You willingly assist when asked.

Initiative – Consider how well the employee seeks and assumes greater responsibility, monitors projects independently, and follows through appropriately.

Unacceptable Superior

☐ 1 ☒ 2 ☐ 3 ☐ 4 ☐ 5

Comments: You've indicated a desire to more and different functions but the inability to organize and accomplish your current duties do not enable you to do this. Improvement is needed in organizing, scheduling, and completing duties in a timely manner.

Adaptability – Consider the ease with which the employee adjusts to any change in duties, procedures, supervisors or work environment. How well does the employee accept new ideas and approaches to work, respond appropriately to constructive criticism and to suggestions for work improvement?

Unacceptable Superior

☐ 1 ☒ 2 ☐ 3 ☐ 4 ☐ 5

Comments: I detect a defensiveness when seeking explanation or information regarding your work load. Your response from our May 11 update meeting was indicative of this temper. I will work with you on evaluating suggestions or ideas but I will not, nor could not, be responsible for making these. I have to rely on you, the individual who does the work, to tell me what will make things more effective and efficient.

Judgment – Consider how well the employee effectively analyzes problems, determines appropriate action for solutions, and exhibits timely and decisive action; thinks logically.

Unacceptable Superior

☐ 1 ☒ 2 ☐ 3 ☐ 4 ☐ 5

Comments: We have discussed issues with the underutilization of your part-time aids to get your duties accomplished. Little intervention is needed from me when you encounter issues but some issues could be prevented with proactive measures—getting the Form 3s verified in a timely way to prevent working with an expired document. Do not wait until the situation is at a critical point before informing me. Come to me with recommendations/suggestions not just problems.

Attendance – Consider number of absences, use of annual and sick leave in accordance with University policy.

☐Unacceptable ☒ Acceptable

Comments:

Punctuality – Consider work arrival and departure in accordance with departmental and University policy.

☐Unacceptable ☒ Acceptable

Comments:

PART III - GOALS/OBJECTIVES/SPECIAL ASSIGNMENTS

Continue to evaluate and refine the Form 3 process to ensure compliance with regulations.

☐ Accomplished or Satisfactory Progress ☒ Unsatisfactory Progress

Comments: We continue to be out of compliance with regulations for Form 3s. I have requested suggestions, ideas, plans, etc. for working toward accomplishing this goal. We have had a critical issue with uncertainty as to whether employees were authorized to work because of expired authorization dates. I am unaware of any preventive measure that has been implemented to avoid these issues.

Develop a policies/procedures manual for your Area.
☐ Accomplished or Satisfactory Progress ☐ Unsatisfactory Progress
Comments: I am unsure about the status of this goal.

Enhance the website regarding Form 3 information, including "do's" and "don'ts", examples, instructions, etc.
☐ Accomplished or Satisfactory Progress ☒ Unsatisfactory Progress
Comments: No additional information has been added to the website to provide those responsible for completing Form 3s in the field with guidance. See Organization A website as an example.

PART IV - OVERALL PERFORMANCE
Unacceptable Superior
☐ 1 ☒ 2 ☐ 3 ☐ 4 ☐ 5
Comments: We have discussed on numerous occasions over the past 12 months, concerns with your Area. We are out of compliance with regulations. The filing of Form As appears to stay reasonably current. The filing of Form Bs and "files not found" information stack up considerably before being addressed. I need from you a plan on how to organize the functions of the Area in order to satisfy the compliance requirements as well as ensure that things are filed and completed in a timely manner. You have worked with Department N to train back up assistance for verifying Form Bs; however, I have received no communication of the effectiveness of this process. Give me a deadline for getting the previous 12 months' Form Bs verified, corrected, and filed. Set a timely for receiving, verifying, correcting, and filing Form Bs on an ongoing basis. Create a plan on how to ensure this is accomplished. Engage Jane Smith in working with you on the Form B website. As we have done over the past year, we will continue to hold monthly meetings to discuss the status of the filing, Form Bs, and other projects.

Exhibit 6a. Sample performance evaluation.

6B. Read the dialogue in Exhibit 6b between a manager, John, and his direct report, Pete. Your task is to assess whether John was thinking like a leader during this interaction. First, assess the underlying organizational purpose and John's actions during the dialogue. Second, assess how the interaction is likely to affect Pete's ego and autonomy needs. Third, predict the effect of this interaction on the relationship between John and Pete. Point to specific examples in the dialogue to support your assessment. Finally, consider whether the effect of this interaction on the leader-member relationship would be different depending on Pete's status as an in-group or out-group member.

John: I'd like to talk with you about building personal relationships. My opinion is that many people don't understand you from a business standpoint or a personal standpoint. For some reason, people have this image of you as being very hard core, controlling, and insensitive, and I don't think that's true.
Pete: Yeah.
John: I think that you're real sensitive, but sometimes you're unwilling to share that sensitivity with others. You need to open yourself up to people because it's a lot easier for them to understand that you're caring and that you want to do what's right for the business and for them.
Pete: With the technicians or team leaders, I always look for their suggestions and their input. I rarely make decisions for people. But somehow the work team sees me this way. The first time I realized it was at our off-site. Smith said he saw me as very controlling, very direct. It shocked me. I went home and told my wife, Peg, and she laughed.
John: [laughs]
Pete: So, to me, it's really two different faces.
John: The other data point I have is that some people outside the department made remarks about your controlling behavior. A group manager said, We ought to put Pete in Industrial Relations to soften him up some."
Pete: [laughs]
John: So, other people have this hard-core image.
Pete: Well, there's probably some validity.
John: You carry a tremendous load for the module. I know you have a lot of irons in the fire, and you work long and hard. I don't want to tell you to stop doing that, but to some degree you have to in order to establish relationships. I think that you can achieve a better balance. In my first three or four years, I was a lot like you. I thought if I wasn't busy, I wasn't contributing. I got a lot of feedback from secretaries especially. I would go in and say, "Here's what I want. Don't ask me how I'm doing today. Don't give me any of this chit-chat about what the weather's like cause I'm here for business. And that's why you're here, too, by the way."
Pete: [laughs]
John: They told me that I acted like they were the lowest people on the totem pole, and I never intended that. But in the way that I behaved, that's the image that they had of me.
Pete: I think I do that with the work team. I guess that's what I'm hearing. [silence]

Exhibit 6b. Leader-member interaction.
(Adapted from Fairhurst & Sarr 1996:104, 118)

7

Going On Record Plainly to Manage Rapport

In the previous chapters, we've focused on thinking like a leader by answering questions that help you assess the management situation using your emotional intelligence to determine the purpose for your intended interaction with a member, its urgency, and your current relationship with that member, along with the potential effect of your action on your future relationship with that member. In the remaining chapters, we're going to turn our attention to using techniques (we'll call them "tactics") for communicating that are best suited to the specific situation—one size does not fit all when it comes to interacting with organizational members. Before I introduce the first communication strategy, I need to briefly describe how your choice of communication strategy helps you manage the quality of your relationships. We're going to talk about "rapport."

Communication and Rapport

Like LMX, rapport is an indicator of relationship quality between individuals. Unlike LMX, rapport is directly tied to the level of enjoyment and sense of personal connection individuals derive from interacting with each other. Thus, rapport is influenced by the specific communication behaviors of individuals. Not surprisingly, research has shown us that rapport is associated with many positive organizational outcomes. For example, stronger rapport between sales representatives and customers increases customer satisfaction, raises the likelihood that the customer will buy in the future, and reduces negative word of mouth. Stronger rapport between managers and subordinates has been connected to better performance and more accurate performance assessments.

Helen Spencer-Oatey coined the term "rapport management" to refer to the use of language to manage relationships. In the TILL system, you will learn to manage rapport—to make interactions more enjoyable for organizational members and create a sense of personal connection with them—by tending to their needs. Chapters 7 through 10 teach you both how and when to use four communication strategies to manage rapport. In this chapter, we'll cover the first one: Going ON RECORD PLAINLY.

Going On Record Plainly

ON RECORD PLAINLY means leaving no doubt as to your message when interacting with a member—your intentions are "on the record" and your meaning is "plain" for all to see. Consider Exhibit 7a.

> TO: Managers
> FROM: Bill Stone, Recruiting Director
> DATE: 1/30/06
> RE: Suggestions for Welcoming New Employees
>
> I suggest using the following techniques for making a new employee feel welcome!
>
> (1) Plan to take the new employee to lunch on their first day. This can be one or two co-workers or the whole team.
> (2) Make sure the new employee begins with all the basic equipment they need to do their job. Complete your request via the Outlook Public Folders as soon as possible.
> (3) Allow the new employee to leave after half a day on their first day. Send them to their drug screen after lunch and send them home. You don't get a lot of production out of anyone on the first day, and you may gain a lot of "loyalty points" instead!
> (4) Assign a "buddy" for the new employee.
> (5) Conduct training immediately, including how to use the phone (voice mail) and email system. Contact Don Warner in IT to schedule training.
> (6) Schedule the new employee to spend some time working on a production line.

Exhibit 7a. An ON RECORD PLAINLY request.

The leader who wrote this memo made his intended action (directing the behavior of his audience) clear. We'll return to this document later. First, I need to show you how to implement the ON RECORD PLAINLY strategy.

How To Use This Strategy

There is a large industry that has grown up around teaching people how to communicate clearly. I will focus here on some simple but effective tactics for going ON RECORD PLAINLY.

Be Explicit and Direct—Using this tactic means stating the action you are attempting to perform as plainly as possible. In Chapter 2, we noted that specific categories of speech acts occur within each category of the COMPETING VALUES FRAMEWORK (Figure 2b). There are several verbs that name speech acts within the four quadrants of the competing values model.

- Informing (representatives): *say*, *tell*, *notify*, *report*, *document*, etc.
- Directing (directives): *request*, *demand*, *insist*, *suggest*, *warn*, etc.
- Consulting (questioning): *ask*, *inquire*, *solicit*, *discuss*, *confer*, etc.
- Valuing (expressives and commissives): *thank*, *appreciate*, *congratulate*, *apologize*, *welcome*, *promise*, *offer*, etc.

These verbs are knows as "performatives" because they allow us to perform the speech act they name when we use the word. For example, the sentence *I apologize for misspelling your name* is not a description of an apology; it itself is an apology. The words constitute the act.

Using this tactic when valuing members of your organization achieves clarity.

- Most clear: *Thank you for your flexibility today* or *I promise you will receive the next available corner office*
- Less clear: *Flexibility is so important right now* or *You're next in line for a corner office*

Similarly, directing a member using this tactic makes your intended action clear.

- Most clear: *I warn you that this behavior will result in suspension in the future*
- Less clear: *This behavior will result in suspension in the future*

Remember that we have not yet taken up the question of when to use the ON RECORD PLAINLY strategy—that comes later in this chapter.

Let's consider Exhibit 7b in which a male upper-level manager in a manufacturing plant is focused on maximizing output. His organizational goal drives him to act by requesting that a female mid-level manager within his organization deal carefully with one of her subordinates who has requested reassignment because of headaches.

Leader: There's no clear justification for this headache thing. I don't know what the solution might be but don't turn a deaf ear to it.
Member: Yeah. I'm not gonna.
Leader: I suggest you differentiate between a safety issue and a work performance issue. Do that real clearly.

Exhibit 7b. Example of ON RECORD PLAINLY : Be Explicit and Direct.
(Adapted from Fairhurst & Chandler 1989:239)

In this situation, the use of the word *suggest* clarifies that the leader's purpose is to direct the member's behavior.

Another tool for making your action explicit involves your choice of sentence structure. Using the imperative form with directive speech acts (as in Exhibit 7b) makes the leader's purpose of directing the member's behavior plain within this dialogue. Note that the leader could have stated the same message using the declarative form. However, the imperative form with the "understood *you*" as subject is the clearest for issuing a directive.

- Most clear: *Do that clearly* (imperative)
- Less clear: *Being real clear is important* (declarative)

Similarly, using the interrogative form when asking a question makes your purpose of consulting explicit, whereas a declarative form (e.g.,) is less plain.

- Most clear: *What's the justification for this headache thing?* (interrogative)
- Less clear: *I wonder what the justification for this headache thing is* (declarative)

Using either the imperative form when directing or the interrogative form when consulting makes your intended action a "direct" speech act.

Be First—Using this tactic means making your intention plain from the outset. There is no "beating around the bush." Consider Exhibit 7c.

Leader: There's no clear justification for this headache thing. I don't know what the solution might be but don't turn a deaf ear to it.
Member: Yeah. I'm not gonna.
Leader: When you write this up, make sure you differentiate between a safety issue and a work performance issue. A safety issue will be defined clearly in our OSHA procedures . . . You might check with Alan to see how he handled that situation with . . .

Exhibit 7c. Example of ON RECORD PLAINLY: Be First.
(Adapted from Fairhurst & Chandler 1989:239)

In Exhibit 7c, the leader's final contribution begins with the leader's direction about differentiating between safety and work performance issues. He offers additional information about how the member might carry out his request—but that information comes after his request (*When you write this up . . .*). What you say (or write) first when interacting with a member is perceived as the most likely "theme" or point of your message.

Be Brief—Using this tactic means being only as informative as needed to get the point of your message across. In other words, you communicate your message with maximum efficiency.

Leader: There's no clear justification for this headache thing. I don't know what the solution might be but don't turn a deaf ear to it.
Member: Yeah. I'm not gonna.
Leader: When you write this up, make sure you differentiate between a safety issue and a work performance issue . . . I remember when this kind of thing just didn't happen. You know, I started working here 22 years ago . . .

Exhibit 7d. Example of failure to use ON RECORD PLAINLY: Be Brief. (Adapted from Fairhurst & Chandler 1989:239)

In Exhibit 7d, the inclusion of historical information in the leader's final contribution makes his purpose (i.e., directing the member's behavior) less plain than in Exhibit 7b, in which his final contribution consists solely of directing statements. Similarly, the leader's final contribution in Exhibit 7d is less clear than in Exhibit 7c, in which he provides information in addition to his request—but that information is directly related to the request.

- Most clear: *I suggest you differentiate between a safety issue and a work performance issue. Do that real clearly*. (Exhibit 7b)
- Less clear: *When you write this up, make sure you differentiate between a safety issue and a work performance issue. A safety issue will be defined clearly in our OSHA procedures . . . You might check with Alan to see how he handled that situation with . . .* (Exhibit 7c)
- Least clear: *When you write this up, make sure you differentiate between a safety issue and a work performance issue . . . I remember when this kind of thing just didn't happen. You know, I started working here 22 years ago . . .* (Exhibit 7d)

Note that giving only needed information also can be accomplished through repetition. For instance, if the leader's final contribution in Exhibit 7d had ended with *now remember to clearly separate safety and work performance*, his message would have been plainer. Note, too, that the Be Brief tactic also applies at the sentence-level: "Be brief" means being concise rather than wordy.

Now let's return to Exhibit 7a, which we looked at briefly at the beginning of this chapter. The writer went ON RECORD PLAINLY in that memo by using all three of the tactics we've just discussed. First, he used the performative verb *suggest* in the very first sentence, and he then used imperative sentence form for each of his six specific suggestions (Be Explicit and Direct tactic) to make his intended action of directing the readers' behavior explicit. Second, he named his intended action in the subject line and the second sentence of the memo (*Plan to take the new employee to lunch*—Be First tactic). Finally, he included only information about these suggestions in the memo (Be Brief tactic). You might note that the leader did one other thing to make his meaning plain. He provided a structure for his information (i.e. a numbered list) that made its "parts" clear. Thus, I need to introduce one final tactic for going ON RECORD PLAINLY.

Be Organized—This tactic is more likely to appear when a leader's message is long or complex. That usually means the leader is writing the message or giving a formal presentation orally. The writer of Exhibit 7a used numbers and a vertical list to arrange his six suggestions, which made his meaning plainer to his audience. In oral situations, speakers provide the same kind of structure by summarizing the information they will present at the beginning of their talk (e.g., *I will cover six suggestions today* . . .) and then by using cues such as *first* or *moving on to the final suggestion* to provide cues when moving from one topic to another.

The four tactics for implementing the ON RECORD PLAINLY strategy in this memo made the leader's intended action and meaning explicit, direct, efficient, and organized (i.e., plain).

When To Use This Strategy

The ON RECORD PLAINLY strategy is effective only in situations in which the organizational purpose is of paramount importance. These situations fall into two categories. In one case, the intended action has positive or neutral effects on rapport with the member. In the second case, the intended action has negative effects on rapport, but that is of less relative importance than the organizational goal. We'll return to Exhibit 7b to evaluate the effectiveness of the leader's communication strategy in his final contribution.

By saying only, *I suggest you differentiate between a safety and a work performance issue. Do that real clearly*, the leader has used three tactics for the ON RECORD PLAINLY strategy in Exhibit 7b: He has made his intended action explicit by using the word *suggest* and the imperative sentence form in *Do that real clearly*; and he has stated only his request with no additional information, which means he has by default stated his intended action first. To judge the effectiveness of that strategy for this interaction, we must first go through the four questions associated with thinking like a leader:

1. What is the organizational purpose driving you to communicate with the member—and how urgent is your need to act? (Chapter 2). The leader's goal is to maximize productivity by directing the member's behavior with her subordinate. The leader's need to act is important but not urgent.
2. Is the member part of your in-group? (Chapter 3). The member is not one of the leader's in-group.
3. How will your message affect the member's ego needs? (Chapter 4). The leader's choice to interact in a face-to-face medium tends the member's ego needs.
4. How will your message affect the member's autonomy needs? (Chapter 5). Directing the member's behavior threatens her autonomy needs (at least to some degree).

The ON RECORD PLAINLY strategy is effective only in situations in which the intended action is urgent or has positive or neutral effects on rapport with the member. This does not accurately describe Exhibit 7b because of the lack of urgency and the threat to the member's autonomy needs. Although the leader's request may not represent a serious imposition, he has still "interfered." After all, the member didn't demonstrate a lack of readiness to handle her task by coming to the leader for advice. Seemingly small impositions by leaders do sometimes convey a lack of trust to members.

If your intended action tends the needs of the member, use of the ON RECORD PLAINLY strategy will be highly effective. For instance, when you want to praise a member (hence tending her ego needs), your message should be as clear as possible. Likewise, when you want to inform a member about a change in procedure (and you've predicted no negative effect to ego or autonomy needs), your message should be as plain as possible. In the case of positive or neutral rapport effects, you make the interaction more enjoyable and create a sense of personal connection when you communicate your message ON RECORD PLAINLY.

In the other case in which going ON RECORD PLAINLY is effective, the intended action has negative effects on rapport with the member but that is deemed of less relative importance than the organizational goal. In Exhibit 7b, it is difficult for me to imagine that the leader's goal of maximizing output is more important than his relationship with the member. And, especially given that the member is not one of the leader's in-group, the leader's choice of this strategy is likely a mistake, showing limited emotional intelligence. Threatening the autonomy of an out-group member when the organizational purpose is not urgent or critical is unwise. Doing it ON RECORD PLAINLY is poor leadership in this case.

There are, of course, situations in which the ON RECORD PLAINLY strategy is effective despite negative rapport effects. For example, when you need to reprimand a member for making inappropriate sexual remarks, your message should be as clear as possible despite the threats to the member's ego or autonomy needs because your message is truly urgent. Such situations, however, will be the exception rather than the rule. Keep in mind that you cannot build human commitment to the organization if you privilege the organization's needs over the member's needs very often. Most of the time, you will want to actively manage rapport by tending to members' needs.

The Bottom Line: Interacting Like a Leader

In the TILL system, you are learning to manage rapport—to make interactions more enjoyable for organizational members and create a sense of personal connection with them—by carefully tending to their needs. The ON RECORD PLAINLY strategy is accomplished by being as clear as possible using four tactics:

Be Explicit and Direct;
Be First;
Be Brief;
Be Organized.

You should use the ON RECORD PLAINLY strategy only when your organizational purpose is of paramount importance or when your intended action has only positive or neutral effects on your member's ego or autonomy needs. This strategy is also effective in those few cases where your intended action is more important than your relationship with the member.

Further Reading

Cutts, M. (1995) *The Quick Reference Plain English Guide*. Oxford: Oxford University Press.

Strunk, Jr., W., and E. B. White (2000) *The Elements of Style,* 4th ed. Needham Heights, MA: Allyn & Bacon.

There are countless books professing to teach you how to be clear. I've listed two here. Although it is less well known, I recommend the first one listed above.

Parker, F. and Riley, K. (2005) *Linguistics for Non-Linguists: A Primer with Exercises, 4th ed.* Boston: Pearson.

This book provides a clear introduction to many of the linguistic concepts underlying the discussion in this chapter. See especially Chapter Two on pragmatics, which covers implicature and speech act theory.

Brown, P. and Levinson, S. C. (1987) *Politeness: Some Universals in Language Usage*. (Studies in Interactional Sociolinguistics, vol. 4). Cambridge: Cambridge University Press.

As mentioned in previous chapters, this book is highly academic but is the primary theoretical work upon which the communication strategy we've covered in Chapter 7 is based. The authors call the strategy "Bald On Record," and their discussion occurs on pages 94-101.

Applications

7A. Read the letter in Exhibit 7e from a manager, Ms. Parker, to one of her organizational members, Ms. Kwon. What is Ms. Parker's organizational purpose and primary action in this letter? What tactics does she use to signal that her purpose is paramount? How effective is she in this management situation? Explain the manager's effectiveness by talking about any predicted changes after delivering this letter to the member.

November 5, 2006
Dear Ms. Kwon,

This letter is to inform you that the condition of the financial records maintained in the storeroom was unacceptable at the end of fiscal year 2006. The FME software system and the FRS general ledger were out of balance over $13,000.00. This is unacceptable. The counter releases were not uploaded for October 31, 2005, December 5, 2005, January 29, 2006, and February 7, 2006. All of the charges for these days had not been charged to other budgets within the organization; therefore, the storeroom had failed to charge out all of these materials. Although you were not responsible for the upload at these times, you were responsible for the integrity of the records. These mistakes caused a tremendous burden of time and effort on my part and the part of others at year end to correct. These types of mistakes won't be tolerated in the future. Please be advised that this is a written warning that further mistakes of this magnitude could result in further disciplinary actions.

Rhonda Parker

Rhonda Parker
Assistant Director

Exhibit 7e. Informational letter regarding financial records.

7B. Read the scene in Exhibit 7f from the film *Lean on Me.* Joe Clark (played by Morgan Freeman) has been hired to take over Eastside High, an inner-city school with very serious problems, and is addressing the faculty and staff for the first time. How would you characterize Clark's purpose? What tactics does he use to signal that his purpose is paramount? How effective is he in this management situation? Explain the manager's effectiveness by talking about any predicted changes in relationship quality and organizational effectiveness after this meeting.

[The scene opens with Mr. Clark being introduced by Mr. O'Malley, the Vice Principal who waxes eloquent welcoming Clark to Eastside.]
Clark: [interrupting] You may sit down, Mr. O'Malley. If you could [run this school] I wouldn't be here, . . . ? No one talks in my meetings. . . . Take out your pencils and write. I want the names of every hoodlum, drug dealer, and miscreant on my desk by noon today. Reverend Slappy . . . you are now the Chief Custodian, . . . You will scour this building clean. Graffiti goes up, it's off the next day. Is that clear?
Slappy: Yes, sir, . . .
Clark: Detention students can help you. Let them scrub this place for awhile. . . . This is my new Dean of Security, Mr. William Wright. He will be my Avenging Angel, as you teachers reclaim the halls. . . . Mr. Zorella, you are now my new Head Football Coach. . . . Mr. Darnell will be your assistant. You know why you're being demoted, Mr. Darnell? Because I'm sick and tired of our football team getting pushed all over the field. Thank you. Sit down. . . . And if you don't like it Mr. Darnell, you can quit. Same goes for the rest of you. You tried it your way for years. And your students can't even get past the Minimum Basic Skills Test. . . . They've given me less than one year . . . to turn this place around . . . so the State will not take us over to perform the tasks which you have failed to do! . . . Forget about the way it used to be. This is not a damn democracy. We are in a state of emergency and my word is law. There's only one boss in this place, and that's me.

Exhibit 7f. Scene from *Lean on Me*.

8
Going Off Record to Manage Rapport

In the previous chapter, you learned about going ON RECORD PLAINLY. To make interactions more enjoyable for organizational members and create a sense of personal connection with them, you must limit the use of that strategy to situations in which either (a) there is no threat to the member's ego or autonomy needs or (b) any threats to the member's needs are less important than your organizational purpose. Clearly, this does not describe all of the situations you must face as a leader.

In this chapter, we'll concentrate on how and when to use the OFF RECORD strategy. Going OFF RECORD means being unclear about your intended actions and making your meaning ambiguous. Exhibit 8a demonstrates the use of the OFF RECORD strategy. The member in this interaction (a male graduate assistant working on the coaching staff of a football team at a state university) consistently arrived at work 45 minutes later than his co-workers. The leader entered the room just as the member was settling into work one morning.

Leader: Hey, how are you guys doing?
Member: Fine. How about you?
Leader: Fine. Have you finished the scouting reports yet?
Member: I am still working on them.
Leader: When you graduate are you wanting to go into coaching?
Member: Yeah.
Leader: Well, when other coaches call me to ask if I know of any graduate assistants that are hardworkers and want to start a coaching career, I could give them your name.
Member: Yeah. [laughing]
Leader: Or I could lie. [Smiling, as he walked out]

Exhibit 8a. An OFF RECORD request.

You can think of the OFF RECORD strategy anchoring the negative end of the clarity continuum and the ON RECORD PLAINLY strategy anchoring the positive end. Thus, in a way, the key to going OFF RECORD is to fail to implement those tactics covered in the previous chapter.

How To Use This Strategy

I'll cover three tactics for implementing this strategy below. These are adapted from the work of H. Paul Grice (1975) on conversational "implicature" and "maxims."

Be Cursory—Using this tactic can mean not interacting with the member at all. There is little that communicates ambiguity as clearly as silence! Think back to Exhibit 3d from the film, *Hunt for Red October*, in which Captain Ramius chooses to ignore the officers sitting around the table with him. Even his silence communicates an intended action and meaning to them. Unfortunately, when you choose to remain silent, the interpretation of your action and meaning is largely beyond your control.

On the other hand, you can use the Be Cursory tactic by providing an insufficient amount of information to make your intended action and meaning clear. Consider Exhibit 8b (similar to one we examined in Chapter 7).

Leader: There's no clear justification for this headache thing. I don't know what the solution might be but don't turn a deaf ear to it.
Member: Yeah. I'm not gonna.
Leader: Differentiating safety and performance issues can be tough.

Exhibit 8b. Example of OFF RECORD: Be Cursory.
(Adapted from Fairhurst & Chandler 1989:239)

In Exhibit 8b, the leader's final contribution provides too little information for the member to recognize that contribution as a request. Rather, the leader hints at what he is directing the member to do using an OFF RECORD strategy. In order to recognize the leader's message as a request, the member will have to create a "bridge" in order to guess at the leader's meaning.

Consider how being cursory influences the clarity of a message intended to value a member.

- Most clear: *Thank you for your flexibility today* (ON RECORD PLAINLY)
- Less clear: *Flexibility is so important* (the Be Cursory tactic for going OFF RECORD)

Similarly, being cursory influences the clarity of a message intended to consult a member.

- Most clear: *I need to know our status* (ON RECORD PLAINLY)
- Less clear: *Status information anyone?* (the Be Cursory tactic for going OFF RECORD)

Be Irrelevant—By giving extraneous information, you obscure the information needed to make your intended action and meaning clear. Consider Exhibit 8c.

Leader: There's no clear justification for this headache thing. I don't know what the solution might be but don't turn a deaf ear to it.
Member: Yeah. I'm not gonna.
Leader: I remember when this kind of thing just didn't happen. You know, I started working here 22 years ago . . . [continues talking about the "good ole days" for several minutes] It's important to differentiate safety and performance issues.

Exhibit 8c. Example of OFF RECORD: Be Irrelevant.
(Adapted from Fairhurst & Chandler 1989:239)

The inclusion of historical information in the leader's final contribution makes his purpose (i.e., directing the member's behavior) ambiguous. He went OFF RECORD by providing too much information.

Be Figurative—Using this tactic means using metaphor or irony rather than being literal when formulating your message.

Leader: There's no clear justification for this headache thing. I don't know what the solution might be but don't turn a deaf ear to it.
Member: Yeah. I'm not gonna.
Leader: Nobody knows how to differentiate between a safety issue and a work performance issue anymore.

Exhibit 8d. Example of OFF RECORD: Be Figurative.
(Adapted from Fairhurst & Chandler 1989:239)

The leader's final contribution makes his purpose (i.e., directing the member's behavior) unclear (i.e. he makes a comment about a distinction "nobody" can make). Instead, the member must guess what the point of the leader's statement has to do with the situation they are currently discussing. The leader's request is OFF RECORD.

Now let's reconsider Exhibit 8a, which we looked at briefly at the beginning of this chapter. The leader went OFF RECORD when reprimanding the member for tardiness by saying, *When coaches call me looking for a hardworking graduate assistant . . . I can give them your name . . . or I can lie*. The leader provided less information than needed to make his intended action (i.e., directing the member's behavior) clear (the Be Cursory tactic). Most strikingly, the coach used irony (we often call this "sarcasm") by saying something the member knows is not literally true (the Be Figurative tactic).

You may be thinking that the leader's reprimand was clear to you when reading Exhibit 8a. While you understood the coach's probable meaning, it's also true that he can rightly claim that he never reprimanded the member. Note that the leader would not have this option if he had gone ON RECORD PLAINLY by saying, *I hereby reprimand you for arriving at work 45 minutes late.* The OFF RECORD communication strategy creates ambiguity in your intended action or meaning.

When To Use This Strategy

The OFF RECORD strategy is effective when your organizational purpose (hence, your intended action) is of negligible importance. Let's continue our discussion of Exhibit 8a. To judge the effectiveness of going OFF RECORD, we must first answer the four questions for thinking like a leader:

1. What is the organizational purpose driving you to communicate with the member—and how urgent is your need to act? (Chapter 2). The leader's goal is to direct the member to get to work on time. His need to act is not urgent.
2. Is the member part of your in-group? (Chapter 3). The member is one of the leader's in-group.
3. How will your message affect the member's ego needs? (Chapter 4). Reprimanding the member threatens his ego needs. Communicating face-to-face tends the member's ego needs.
4. How will your message affect the member's autonomy needs? (Chapter 5). Dictating when the member should arrive at work threatens his autonomy needs.

There are two possible situations in which the OFF RECORD strategy can be used. In the first, the leader is the initiator and the organizational purpose is unimportant. This might be the case in Exhibit 8a. However, if the coach had determined that his intended action of directing the member's behavior was unimportant, it seems his smartest move would have been to go OFF RECORD by remaining silent (Be Cursory). On the other hand, if the coach had determined that his organizational purpose was important, the OFF RECORD strategy would not be appropriate because of the ambiguity it creates.

In the second situation, the organizational purpose is unimportant, but the member initiates the interaction; so, the leader's need to act is urgent. This is clearly not the case in Exhibit 8a. However, this type of situation might occur when a member is completing a task using a technique that is adequate but that you do not personally like. If the member prompts you to comment on the technique, you are "trapped" in the sense that you must respond even if you are hesitant to do anything to threaten the rapport between the two of you. If your desire to critique the member's technique is unimportant at present, you might go OFF RECORD by understating your opinion: *I'm glad it's working for you.* Note that going OFF RECORD is different from lying to the member about your opinion.

So how effective is the leader's sarcasm in Exhibit 8a? It is important to remember the dialogue occurs between males working on the coaching staff of a college football team. It turns out that the more roles are held in a rigid hierarchy within an organization, the more effective is the OFF RECORD strategy. If you think back to the discussion of cultural values from Chapter 5, organizations with a culture embracing high power distance are likely to find the OFF RECORD strategy appropriate because of their assumption that those with little power are responsible for figuring out how to serve those with greater power.

Deborah Tannen shares the following story from a former Navy man about clarity in the military:

> Many years ago, when I was in the Navy, I was training to be a radio technician. One class I was in was taught by a Chief Radioman, a regular Navy man who had been to sea, and who was then in his third hitch. The students, about twenty of us, were fresh out of boot camp, with no sea duty, and little knowledge of real Navy life. One day in class the Chief said it was hot in the room. The students didn't react, except perhaps to nod in agreement. The Chief repeated himself: "It's hot in this room." Again there was no reaction from the students.
>
> Then the Chief explained. He wasn't looking for agreement or discussion from us. When he said that the room was hot, he expected us to do something about it—like opening the window. He tried it one more time, and this time all of us left our work benches and headed for the windows. And we had many opportunities to apply what we had learned. (1994: 87)

It is precisely because of the rigid hierarchy that the leader in this case expected the members to fix the problem he noted. The Air Force officers with whom I used to work told me a "direct order" (i.e., use of the ON RECORD PLAINLY strategy) was very rare and usually indicated a reprimand rather than a simple request.

Based on the rigid hierarchy of a football organization, I believe the coach's sarcasm in Exhibit 8a was an effective tactic for reprimanding the graduate assistant in the current situation. It will be necessary for the coach to use a less ambiguous strategy to communicate the reprimand if the problem becomes more urgent in the future.

To sum up, even if you work within a rigid hierarchy, you should use the OFF RECORD strategy only when your organizational purpose is of little importance. This should be a fairly rare occurrence. In addition, you should use the Be Irrelevant tactic and the Be Figurative tactic only when you are certain the member is one of your in-group.

The Bottom Line: Interacting Like a Leader

The OFF RECORD strategy is accomplished by making your intended actions and meaning ambiguous using three tactics:

- Be Cursory;
- Be Irrelevant;
- Be Figurative.

To manage rapport (to make interactions more enjoyable for organizational members and create a sense of personal connection), you should use the OFF RECORD strategy sparingly. Because most North American organizations have become "flatter," the use of the OFF RECORD strategy is less effective than in the past because those with less power are not held responsible for figuring out how to serve those with greater power. In other words, as organizational members are treated more as equals, it becomes more unlikely that opaque messages will be interpreted as directives.

Further Reading

Tannen, D. (1994) Talking From 9 to 5: Women and Men in the Workplace: Language, Sex and Power. New York: Avon Books.
This book is an interesting treatment of gender differences in talk at work. Chapter Two discusses conversation rituals and includes a description of "ritual fighting" and "teasing" as typical among American males.

Fairhurst, G. T. and Sarr, R. A. (1996) *The Art of Framing: Managing the Language of Leadership*. San Francisco: Jossey-Bass.
Fairhurst and Sarr's book includes a description of how figurative language helps leaders influence the perceptions of subordinates. Chapter Five contains some interesting examples of metaphor in leader's dialogues.

Parker, F. and Riley, K. (2005) *Linguistics for Non-Linguists: A Primer with Exercises, 4th ed.* Boston: Pearson.

This book provides a clear introduction to many of the linguistic concepts underlying the discussion in this chapter. See especially Chapter Two on pragmatics, which covers implicature and speech act theory.

Brown, P. and Levinson, S. C. (1987) *Politeness: Some Universals in Language Usage*. (Studies in Interactional Sociolinguistics, vol. 4). Cambridge: Cambridge University Press.

As mentioned previously, this book is highly academic but is also the primary theoretical work upon which the communication strategy we've covered in Chapter 8 is based. The authors discuss the OFF RECORD strategy on pages 211-227.

Applications

8A. To practice identifying the OFF RECORD strategy, consider the interaction between two male co-workers at an advertising agency in Tokyo in Exhibit 8e. Ember is an American copywriter who has created some English copy for an ad that was developed in Japanese, and Nakada is an account executive with slightly more power than the copywriter within this situation. Nakada's organizational goal was to inform Ember that the ad copy he created had been rejected for use.

Ember: I mean you can see through it, right? You don't have to use your imagination. You can see every little thing. So it plays off of the visual—leaves nothing to the imagination.
Nakada: Is that so? [pause] The idea is very clear to me now. This video can do everything. But too much pitch for the visual.
Ember: Too much? No. no.
Nakada: Too much visual. No?
Ember: No. No. I don't think so.
Nakada: Maybe.
Ember: Maybe?
Nakada: Yeah.
Ember: I think it's okay.
Nakada: Let's think about it.

Exhibit 8e. Example of OFF RECORD tactics.
(Adapted from Miller 2000:246-247)

What is Ember's intended action within this interaction? How is rapport between the co-workers potentially threatened? Which OFF RECORD tactics does Nakada use? Is this strategy successful? Explain using specific examples.

8B. Consider the interaction from *Working Girl* in Exhibit 8f. The leader, Katherine (played by Sigourney Weaver), is approached by a new assistant named Tess (played by Melanie Griffith). What is Tess's intended action in this situation? What is the Katherine's intended action? How is leader-member rapport potentially threatened? Which OFF RECORD tactics does Katherine use? Is this strategy successful in this situation? Explain using specific examples.

Tess: You said I could come to you [if I had an idea].
Katherine: Shoot.
Tess: You know how Trask Industries has been looking to buy into broadcasting? [Well] all of a sudden I thought, "radio."
Katherine: [They're] looking for television stations.
Tess: So is [everyone else]. See, my idea is that they [start with] radio . . . [for one thing] there's a lot more of them for sale. Plus it would solve Trask's problem with [the] Japanese trying to take him over, because FCC forbids foreign ownership of radio as well as TV.
Katherine: Interesting. You've been . . . following this . . . ?
Tess: Yeah.
Katherine: No chance you overheard it, say, in the elevator?
Tess: No. . . . It's my idea.
Katherine: Good. . . . Discuss it with anyone . . . ?
Tess: Nope. You think . . . there's something there?
Katherine: Well . . . Why don't you leave me your notes and I'll have a look-see.
Tess: Okay. Um, I've been trying to get into the Entre Program, and this would [help]. I mean if anything. . . happens, you'll remember . . . .
Katherine: Absolutely, Tess.

Exhibit 8f. Example of OFF RECORD tactics from *Working Girl*.

9

Tending Ego Needs:
Going On Record Politely to Manage Rapport

At this point, you have learned what to do to manage rapport when you face a situation in which your organizational purpose is paramount (Chapter 7) or negligible (Chapter 8). We'll now begin to consider the more common situation faced by organizational leaders: to achieve balance in situations where both organizational purpose and member relationships are crucial. You will learn ON RECORD POLITELY communication strategies to manage rapport by achieving such a balance.

There are two ON RECORD POLITELY strategies:

- TENDING EGO NEEDS (Chapter 9)
- TENDING AUTONOMY NEEDS (Chapter 10)

Both are based on tending to the needs of members as outlined earlier in this book. For now, we'll concentrate on *how* and *when* to use the TENDING EGO NEEDS strategy. In the TILL system of effective communication, attending to the ego needs of members is akin to tending the plants in a garden by providing fertilizer. The "tending" is how you ensure maximum growth for each individual plant and the garden as a whole. You can, of course, ignore the individual plant's need for fertilizer in the same way you can ignore the ego needs of members in your organization. In both cases, however, you are "threatening" the health of the individual, as well as the entire collective.

Consider Exhibit 9a, a conversation which took place during a product development meeting between a male team leader and a male team member who works as a product engineer. Although the engineer believes more marketing information is needed on the product their team is developing, the team leader informs him the client's wishes are more important than the team's desire to design the best possible product.

Member: Um, I'm still real concerned about this spray guard thing [conversation continues for several minutes] I mean . . . do we feel good about it? If six people wear this in Germany, wear this respirator product, is that enough? I don't know, I mean how do YOU feel about it?
Leader: I feel like it increases the risk, I always have, but I think we have to . . . you know, it's their product and we have to trust them. There's an element of

trust there. I mean, like you say, they're happy with it. I guess we have to accept that; I mean we . . .

Exhibit 9a. Example of ON RECORD POLITELY: TENDING EGO NEEDS . (Donnellon 1996:175-176)

The leader disagrees with the member clearly but politely. Going ON RECORD POLITELY means making your intended action and meaning less clear than ON RECORD PLAINLY but more clear than OFF RECORD. We'll return to this dialogue later. First, I need to show you how to implement this strategy.

How To Use This Strategy

In Chapter 4, I noted that leaders tend to members' ego needs (and build organizational commitment) by making decisions that demonstrate the positive value of those members to the organization. The three tactics for implementing the TENDING EGO NEEDS strategy reflect communication choices which support the member's ego needs.

Be Positive—Using this tactic means signaling that you value the member. One simple way to demonstrate that value is to address the member by name. Second person pronouns (e.g., *you*, *your*, etc.) and positive statements about the member (e.g., *I was impressed with your work on that project* or *I'm so glad to have an engineer on the team*) are the most common ways to acknowledge the member's value. This is sometimes called adopting a "you-perspective."

Let's return to the dialogue we've been considering in the last few chapters in which a male upper-level manager is focused on maximizing output. His organizational goal drives him to act by requesting that a female mid-level manager deal carefully with one of her subordinates who has requested reassignment because of headaches.

Leader: There's no clear justification for this headache thing. I don't know what the solution might be but don't turn a deaf ear to it.
Member: Yeah. I'm not gonna.
Leader: I liked the way you differentiated between a safety issue and a work performance issue the last time this kind of thing came up.

Exhibit 9b. Example of ON RECORD POLITELY: TENDING EGO NEEDS: Be Positive. (Adapted from Fairhurst & Chandler 1989:239)

The leader's final contribution attempts to influence the member by praising the way she handled a similar situation in the past. The leader's communication strategy tends to the ego needs of the member and is thus more polite but less clear than his ON RECORD PLAINLY strategy in Exhibit 7b. On the other hand, the leader's intended purpose and meaning is clearer than when going OFF RECORD by discussing his history with the company, as in Exhibit 8c.

- Most clear: *I suggest you differentiate between a safety issue and a work performance issue* (ON RECORD PLAINLY)
- Moderately clear: *I liked the way you differentiated between a safety issue and a work performance issue the last time this kind of thing came up* (ON RECORD POLITELY: TENDING EGO NEEDS)
- Least clear: *I remember when this kind of thing just didn't happen. You know, I started working here 22 years ago . . .* [continues talking about the "good ole days" for several minutes] *It's important to differentiate safety and performance issues* (OFF RECORD)

This is an appropriate time to note that any form of criticism from a leader must focus clearly on a member's behavior—not the member—in order to mitigate the negative effect of the criticism. For instance, consider the dialogue below between a female supervisor and her male subordinate.

Leader: You are always late. Some people in your department think you are lazy.
Member: I am not lazy. If you think that, you don't understand me at all.

Exhibit 9c. Example of leader criticizing member without TENDING EGO NEEDS. (McKirchy 1998:10)

In Exhibit 9c, the leader focuses on the member by calling him *lazy*. Compare the alternate version of this dialogue in Exhibit 9d.

Leader: You need to focus on being here on time. Some of your customers call you at 8 a.m. and you're not here to take care of them.
Member: You're right. I can't get the same level of sales from them as from my other customers. Maybe that's the reason.

Exhibit 9d. Example of leader criticizing member while TENDING EGO NEEDS. (Adapted from McKirchy 1998:11)

In Exhibit 9d, the leader focuses on specific behavior (i.e., *being here on time*) as opposed to an inherent quality of the member (i.e., *You are lazy*). In addition, the leader implies the positive value of the member by presuming that the member would be able to handle the needs of his customers if he were there when they called. In other words, the leader manages rapport by signaling that the criticism is not an indication of the value of the member to the organization.

Be Inclusive—Using the second tactic for TENDING EGO NEEDS means signaling that you and the member are part of the same group by using in-group markers. First person inclusive pronouns (e.g., *we*, *our*, etc.), shared jargon, slang, or dialect (e.g., *y'all* or *the SUPe store*), and endearments (e.g., *Bobby* for *Robert* or *sister*) are the most common linguistic signals of in-group status. For example, the leader uses *we* in his final comment in Exhibit 9e.

Leader: There's no clear justification for this headache thing. I don't know what the solution might be but don't turn a deaf ear to it.
Member: Yeah. I'm not gonna.
Leader: We need to differentiate clearly between a safety issue and a work performance issue.

Exhibit 9e. Example of ON RECORD POLITELY: TENDING EGO NEEDS: Be Inclusive. (Adapted from Fairhurst & Chandler 1989:239)

Using the Be Inclusive tactic when informing members of your organization means making your action polite but relatively clear.

- Most clear: *I disagree that more information will make this problem easier to solve* (ON RECORD PLAINLY)
- Moderately clear: *Bobby, we know more information won't make this problem easier to solve* (TENDING EGO NEEDS by Being Inclusive)
- Least clear: *It's true information is pow*er (OFF RECORD)

Similarly, this tactic can make your message both clear and polite when consulting a member.

- Most clear: *I need to know our status* (ON RECORD PLAINLY)
- Moderately clear: *I wonder what our status is?* (TENDING EGO NEEDS by Being Inclusive)
- Least clear: *Status information anyone?* (OFF RECORD)

Once again, we will not take up the question of when to use the TENDING EGO NEEDS strategy until later in this chapter.

Be Present—Effective listening is active not passive; it requires conscious effort and considerable skill. In other words, listening is not the same as remaining silent while others talk. I noted in the previous chapter that the meaning of silence is ambiguous. In contrast, the meaning of active listening is clear: You demonstrate that you value the speaker by giving your time and attention to that person.

You signal that you are listening during a conversation when you make eye contact, nod your head, and use verbal fillers like *uh huh* or *I see*. Perhaps the most powerful signal of active listening is rephrasing what you have heard in your own words. As an example, consider the memo in Exhibit 9f, which originally appeared in Chapter 1. Earlier, I noted that this document is a leadership (as opposed to management) message because the writer focuses on relationships rather than tasks. The leader's use of the Be Present tactic for the TENDING EGO NEEDS strategy (i.e., summarizing the audience's previous comments) is what signals that relationship focus.

Now let's reconsider Exhibit 9a from the beginning of this chapter. The leader went ON RECORD POLITELY by TENDING EGO NEEDS when disagreeing with the member by saying *we have to trust them* and *we have to accept that* (Be Inclusive tactic). In addition, he lets the member know he has been listening by saying *like you say they're happy with it* (Be Present tactic).

TO: Managers
FROM: Bill Stone, Human Resource Director
DATE: 7/28/06
RE: Results of the Recruiting Survey

In February, we sent out a survey of our recruiting process to get ideas and suggestions for improving our service to you. Thank you all for taking the time to respond to the survey. The information we gained was very helpful.

Many of you said you have been happy with the results you have seen and have been glad to no longer have to manage recruiting yourselves. The positive feedback was very encouraging. However, now that we have some basic processes in place, we realize that improvement is the next step. Based on your responses, we will be taking several steps this year to make our service even better:

* Working to decrease the time to fill a position using the Human Resource Assistant for administrative areas of recruiting.

* Researching and implementing more automation to further decrease the time to fill a position. Through technology we hope to have a better system of handling candidate flow and reporting of recruiting activities.

* Updating the career section of our organizational website and increasing recruiting resources available there.

* Communicating more proactively with managers to determine departmental forecasting and goals. I hope to meet with all of you periodically to discuss your plans.

Exhibit 9f. Example of ON RECORD POLITELY: TENDING EGO NEEDS.

When To Use This Strategy

The ON RECORD POLITELY: TENDING EGO NEEDS strategy is effective in situations in which both organizational purpose and member relationships are crucial. We'll return to Exhibit 9a to evaluate the effectiveness this strategy. We must first answer the four questions associated with thinking like a leader:

1. What is the organizational purpose driving you to communicate with the member—and how urgent is your need to act? (Chapter 2). The leader's goal is to inform the member from engineering that the leader disagrees with the member's desire to collect more marketing information on the product under development. His goal does not appear to be urgent.
2. Is the member part of your in-group? (Chapter 3). We'll assume the member is not one of the leader's in-group.
3. How will your message affect the member's ego needs? (Chapter 4). Disagreeing with the member threatens his ego needs. However, choosing to interact with the member in a face-to-face situation tends his ego needs.
4. How will your message affect the member's autonomy needs? (Chapter 5). Autonomy needs do not appear to be an issue in this situation.

The TENDING EGO NEEDS strategy is effective in situations in which both your organizational purpose (hence, your intended action) and your rapport with a member are important. These situations are probably the most common ones you face as a leader. This certainly appears to describe the situation in Exhibit 9a: The leader wants to persuade the member that getting additional marketing information to design a better product isn't warranted because the client is happy with the quality of the current product. Although he needs to communicate his disagreement with the engineer, he doesn't want to do anything to lower the quality of his relationship with him—especially because the engineer is not part of the leader's in-group. Note also that the leader disagrees in a face-to-face meeting, which tends to the member's ego needs more than other forms of communication media. Thus, the leader's choice of the TENDING EGO NEEDS strategy is effective in the case of Exhibit 9a.

It's hard to go wrong with the TENDING EGO NEEDS strategy except in two situations. First, it's a mistake to express interest in the member (Be Positive tactic) when you are not sincere. Don't fool yourself—people (especially the members within your organization) know. Second, it's a mistake to refer to the member as one of your in-group (Be Inclusive tactic) unless you are certain the member really is. (Remember you are likely to overestimate the quality of your relationships with members.) In both of these situations, you will end up sounding insincere and undermine any effort to tend to your relationship. In contrast, actively listening (Be Present tactic) is always appropriate for tending to ego needs in any situation in which you need to balance organizational goals and relationships.

You should use the ON RECORD POLITELY: TENDING EGO NEEDS strategy when both your organizational purpose and your relationship with a member are important. This should describe most of the situations in which you interact with members. In contrast, if your intended action poses no threat to your rapport with the member, you should be using the ON RECORD PLAINLY strategy instead.

The Bottom Line: Interacting Like a Leader

The ON RECORD POLITELY: TENDING EGO NEEDS strategy is accomplished by making your intended actions and meaning clear but polite by using three tactics:

- Be Positive;
- Be Inclusive;
- Be Present.

You should use this strategy to manage rapport when your organizational purpose is important but threatening to the member and your relationship with that member is also important. There are two cautionary notes about the use of this strategy: You must be sincere when signaling the value of the member; and the member must actually be part of your in-group if you use in-group markers.

Further Reading

Steil, L. K. and Bommelje, R.K. (2004) *Listening Leaders: The Ten Golden Rules to Listen, Lead and Succeed.* Edina, MN: Beavers Pond Press.

This book is a comprehensive treatment of listening for leaders and includes discussion of the SIER process for effective listening: (a) Sensing, (b) Interpreting, (c) Evaluating, and (d) Responding.

Brown, P. and Levinson, S. C. (1987) *Politeness: Some Universals in Language Usage.* (Studies in Interactional Sociolinguistics, vol. 4). Cambridge: Cambridge University Press.

Although this book is highly academic, it is the primary theoretical work upon which the communication strategy we've covered in Chapter 9 is based. The authors call this strategy "positive politeness," and their discussion occurs on pages 101-129.

Applications

9A. Read the interactions below from the film *Mr. Holland's Opus* between a music teacher (played by Richard Dreyfuss) and his students during two class meetings. In Exhibit 10f, Mr. Holland is returning a set of recent tests. The interaction in Exhibit 10g occurs with the same set of students a few weeks later. Your task is to analyze the management situation in each case (i.e., What is Mr. Holland's intended action in each situation? How is leader-member rapport potentially threatened in each situation?). Which ON RECORD POLITELY: TENDING EGO NEEDS tactics does Mr. Holland use in each situation? Is he successful? Explain using specific examples.

Holland: These tests are pathetic. [reading from the paper in his hand] Name an American composer. Ms. Swedland, your answer was . . . [looks at her]
Ms. Swedland: Bach.
Holland: Johann Sebastian Bach. [looking through papers in his hand] . . . This is my favorite. How do you know what key a concerto is in? Mr. Mims. Your answer was "Look on the front page—."[pause] [Holland continues berating students] These tests are a complete waste of my time AND yours!
Mr. Sullivan: [whispering to another classmate nearby] . . . . I'd rather be anywhere else.
Holland: Mr. Sullivan, why don't you pay a visit to Mr. Waters . . . . Get your books and get OUT [pointing at door] The rest . . . . get your textbooks out. We're going to go over these questions. . . . Until you get them right.

Exhibit 9g. Interaction from *Mr. Holland's Opus*.

Holland: Can [anyone] tell me the difference between the Ionian and Dorian scales? [pauses for several seconds and then chuckles quietly] I just wanted to confirm that I've made absolutely no impact on you. [smiling] Mr. Sullivan, what kind of music do you like . . . ? [silence] Don't be afraid.
Mr. Sullivan: Rock-n-roll.
Holland: What about you?
Student 1: Classical.
Holland: [looking at the rest of the students] Brown-noser. [smiling] [students laugh] [sits at piano and begins playing a contemporary tune] What's this called?
Student 2: Lover's Concerto[by] The Toys.
Holland: Wrong! [continues playing] That's Minuet in G. . . . written by Johann Sebastian Bach. . . . in 1725. They are both prime examples of the Ionian scale. Now listen.

Exhibit 9h. Another interaction from *Mr. Holland's Opus*.

9B. Revisit the dialogue in Exhibit 9i from the film, *Working Girl*, as well as your answer to Application 5A about the management situation. Can you identify any ON RECORD POLITELY: TENDING EGO NEEDS tactics used by either of the managers? Are those tactics successful? Why or why not? Rewrite at least two of their contributions using different TENDING EGO NEEDS tactics to make them more effective leaders in this situation.

Mr. Turkel: Tess, I have some good news and some bad news . . . they turned you down for the Entre Program again.
Tess: Why?
Mr. Lutz: We did all we could, Tessy.
Mr. Turkel: I mean, you have to remember, you're up against Harvard and Wharton graduates. What do you got? Some night school, some secretarial time on your sheet?
Mr. Lutz: Christians and lions, Tess. . . .
Tess: And the good news?
Mr. Lutz: Bob in Arbitrage. You're so hungry. They're looking for hungry down there!
Tess: Really?
Mr. Lutz: . . . Bob's looking for a new assistant and wants to meet you for a drink.
Tess: This isn't another set-up?
Mr. Lutz: Do I look like a pimp? Bob says he's looking for hungry, I think to myself, "Tess." . . .
Tess: Bob in Arbitrage.
Mr. Lutz: Bob Speck. Extension 256. He's expecting your call. Go get 'em, Tessy!

Exhibit 9i. Interaction from *Working Girl*.

10

Tending Autonomy Needs: Going On Record Politely to Manage Rapport

In the previous chapter, you learned about going ON RECORD POLITELY by TENDING EGO NEEDS. To make interactions more enjoyable for organizational members and create a sense of personal connection with them, you must limit the use of that strategy to situations in which (a) your organizational purpose is important, and (b) you want to mitigate threats to the member's ego needs. Because you will also face situations in which you want to mitigate threats to the member's autonomy needs, we'll concentrate on how and when to use the TENDING AUTONOMY NEEDS strategy in this chapter.

In the TILL system, attending to the autonomy needs of members is akin to tending the plants in a garden by providing adequate space so that each plant gets sufficient sunlight. The "tending" is how you ensure growth of each individual plant and the garden as a whole. You can, of course, ignore the individual plant's need for space in the same way you can ignore the autonomy needs of members in your organization. In both cases, however, you threaten the health of the individual, as well as the entire collective.

Consider the memo in Exhibit 10a, which was sent by the HR director to the managers within his organization. (I presented a different version of this memo in Exhibit 7a.) The writer directs the future actions of the audience clearly but politely.

TO: Managers
FROM: Bill Stone, Recruiting Director
DATE: 1/30/06
RE: Suggestions for Welcoming New Employees

I would be grateful if all managers would consider the suggestions below for making a new employee feel welcome!

(1) Plan to take the new employee to lunch on their first day. This can be one or two co-workers or the whole team.
(2) Make sure the new employee begins with all the basic equipment they need to do their job. Complete your request via the Outlook Public Folders as soon as possible.
(3) Allow the new employee to leave after half a day on their first day. Send them to their drug screen after lunch and send them home. You don't get a lot of production out of anyone on the first day, and you may gain a lot of "loyalty points" instead!
(4) Assign a "buddy" for the new employee.
(5) Conduct training immediately, including how to use the phone (voice mail) and email system. Contact Don Warner in IT to schedule training.
(6) Schedule the new employee to spend some time working on a production line.

I apologize if this sounds overwhelming, but using some of these suggestions will insure our organization is THE employer of choice.

Exhibit 10a. A request illustrating ON RECORD POLITELY: TENDING AUTONOMY NEEDS.

To repeat, going ON RECORD POLITELY means making your intended action and meaning less clear than ON RECORD PLAINLY but more clear than OFF RECORD. We'll return to this memo later in this chapter. At this point, I need to show you how to implement the TENDING AUTONOMY NEEDS strategy.

How To Use This Strategy

In Chapter 5, I noted that leaders tend to members' autonomy needs by demonstrating that they respect those members' freedom to act as they choose. The seven tactics for implementing the TENDING AUTONOMY NEEDS strategy reflect communication choices which acknowledge the member's freedom of action.

Question or Hedge—Using the first tactic to make your directive both clear and polite means using an interrogative sentence form (i.e., posing your request as a question) and/or using a hedge (eg. *possibly*).

- Most clear: *Submit your report on Friday* (ON RECORD PLAINLY)
- Moderately clear: *Can you submit your report on Friday?* (Question tactic for TENDING AUTONOMY NEEDS)
- Least clear: *It would be nice to have your report on Friday* (OFF RECORD)

Similarly, you can use this tactic by hedging when you inform a member.

- Most clear: *Your deadline is fixed* (ON RECORD PLAINLY)
- Moderately clear: *I suspect your deadline is fixed* (Hedge tactic for TENDING AUTONOMY NEEDS)
- Least clear: *It would be hard to move the deadline* (OFF RECORD)

Finally, you use this tactic by hedging when you value a member.

- Most clear: *Thank you for your flexibility today* (ON RECORD PLAINLY)
- Moderately clear: *I think your flexibility is important today* (Hedge tactic for TENDING AUTONOMY NEEDS)
- Least clear: *Flexibility is so important* (OFF RECORD)

If you are thinking that the examples above contrasting TENDING AUTONOMY NEEDS with ON RECORD PLAINLY aren't all that different, you would be correct. I noted earlier that the OFF RECORD strategy anchors the negative end of the clarity continuum, while the ON RECORD PLAINLY strategy anchors the positive end. Both ON RECORD POLITELY strategies appear near the middle of the continuum, but TENDING AUTONOMY NEEDS is a little clearer than TENDING EGO NEEDS. At this point, you've probably noticed that clarity and politeness are inversely related. Figure 10a displays the communication strategies in the TILL system on a clarity/politeness continuum.

Figure 10a. The clarity/politeness continuum.

TENDING AUTONOMY NEEDS is often called "conventional politeness." More specifically, the use of tactics for implementing this strategy (e.g., questioning or hedging) are so commonplace that they signal only a slight nod to autonomy needs and are, therefore, only a little more polite than going ON RECORD PLAINLY. Despite this fact, each generation of parents continues to teach their children to say *please* when making requests because failure to do so signals a noticeable breach of etiquette.

Be Impersonal—Using the second tactic means being both clear and polite by using passive voice and/or avoiding the word *you*.

- Most clear: *Submit your report on Friday* (ON RECORD PLAINLY)
- Moderately clear: *Reports should be submitted on Friday* (Be Impersonal tactic for TENDING AUTONOMY NEEDS)
- Least clear: *It would be nice to have reports on Friday* (OFF RECORD)

You can accomplish the same balance between clarity and politeness when using this tactic while informing a member.

- Most clear: *Your deadline is fixed* (ON RECORD PLAINLY)
- Moderately clear: *The deadline is fixed* (Be Impersonal tactic for TENDING AUTONOMY NEEDS)
- Least clear: *It would be hard to move the deadline* (OFF RECORD)

The dialogue in Exhibit 10b also illustrates the use of the Be Impersonal tactic.

Leader: There's no clear justification for this headache thing. I don't know what the solution might be but don't turn a deaf ear to it.
Member: Yeah. I'm not gonna.
Leader: Safety and performance issues should be differentiated in this case.

Exhibit 10b. Example of ON RECORD POLITELY: TENDING AUTONOMY NEEDS: Be Impersonal. (Adapted from Fairhurst & Chandler 1989:239)

The leader's final contribution tends to the autonomy needs of the member by expressing his directions impersonally (i.e., the member is not explicitly named). Thus, the leader's communication strategy is more polite but less clear than his ON RECORD PLAINLY strategy in Exhibit 7b (i.e., *I suggest you differentiate. . .*).

Minimize—Using the third tactic means being both clear and polite by downplaying the imposition of a request.

- Most clear: *Submit your report on Friday this week.* (ON RECORD PLAINLY)

- Moderately clear: *I need your report on Friday this week, just this once.* (Minimize tactic for TENDING AUTONOMY NEEDS)
- Least clear: *It would be nice to have your report on Friday this week.* (OFF RECORD)

It can also be used when consulting a member.

- Most clear: *When did the customer first call?* (ON RECORD PLAINLY)
- Moderately clear: *I have a quick question about the timing of that first call* (Minimize tactic for TENDING AUTONOMY NEEDS)
- Least clear: *The timing of that first call is important* (OFF RECORD)

Be Deferential—Using the fourth tactic means being both clear and polite by elevating the status of the member or lowering your own status.

- Most clear: *Submit your report on Friday* (ON RECORD PLAINLY)
- Moderately clear: *Because I'm a novice at this, I'll need your report on Friday* (Be Deferential tactic for TENDING AUTONOMY NEEDS)
- Least clear: *It would be nice to have your report on Friday* (OFF RECORD)

In the example above, you show deference to the member by lowering your own status (i.e., you threaten your own ego needs by calling yourself *a novice*). You can also show deference by using "honorific" terms, where appropriate, like *sir* or titles like *professor*, *judge*, *Mr. Chairman*, *your honor*, and so on.

You may see the use of such terms as problematic. Because of the relative social equality of individuals in Western cultures, the Be Deferential tactic is perhaps less common than in cultures which maintain more social stratification and thus expect more deference. However, the use of *sir* and *ma'am* is still common in parts of the U.S., and there are two forms of the second-person pronoun *you* in French and Spanish specifically for showing deference when addressing someone with higher social status, including strangers. Both cultures are certainly "Western" so that we cannot simply ignore this tactic. On the other hand, most languages in Eastern Asia (e.g., Japanese, Chinese, and Korean) have a fairly complex system of honorifics that must be learned in order to show appropriate deference.

Be Pessimistic—Using the fifth tactic means being both clear and polite by expressing doubt *(e.g., could, might, I don't suppose)* while directing a member.

- Most clear: *Submit your report on Friday* (ON RECORD PLAINLY)
- Moderately clear: *You might submit your report on Friday* (Be Pessimistic tactic for TENDING AUTONOMY NEEDS)

- Least clear: *It would be nice to have your report on Friday* (OFF RECORD)

Similarly, you can use this tactic when informing a member.

- Most clear: *The deadline is fixed* (ON RECORD PLAINLY)
- Moderately clear: *The deadline could be fixed* (Be Pessimistic tactic for TENDING AUTONOMY NEEDS)
- Least clear: *It would be hard to move the deadline* (OFF RECORD)

This tactic can be a form of conventional politeness, signaling a minimal acknowledgement of autonomy needs, but your sincerity can make this tactic more powerful. For instance, review the dialogue in Exhibit 10a.

Leader: There's no clear justification for this headache thing. I don't know what the solution might be but don't turn a deaf ear to it.
Member: Yeah. I'm not gonna.
Leader: I'm not sure it will be possible, but if you can, differentiate clearly between safety and performance issues.

Exhibit 10c. Example of ON RECORD POLITELY: TENDING AUTONOMY NEEDS: Be Pessimistic. (Adapted from Fairhurst & Chandler 1989:239)

Note that the leader's final contribution tends to the autonomy needs of the member by expressing his directive with pessimism rather than certainty (i.e., *I'm not sure it will be possible* and *if you can . . .*). If the leader's pessimism about this task is sincere, his use of this tactic is more powerful because the leader is truly tending to the autonomy needs of the member by allowing her to determine whether the directive can be carried out. On the other hand, if the leader's pessimism is only conventional, then his use of this tactic is only slightly more polite/less clear than his ON RECORD PLAINLY strategy in Exhibit 7b (i.e., *I suggest you differentiate . . .*).

Apologize—Using the sixth tactic means being both clear and polite by including an apology while directing a member.

- Most clear: *Submit your report on Friday* (ON RECORD PLAINLY)
- Moderately clear: *I'm sorry but I need your report on Friday* (Apologize tactic for TENDING AUTONOMY NEEDS)
- Least clear: *It would be nice to have your report on Friday* (OFF RECORD)

Similarly, you can use this tactic when consulting a member.

- Most clear: *When did the customer first call?* (ON RECORD PLAINLY)

- Moderately clear: *I hate to ask you, but can you tell me when the customer first called?* (Apologize tactic for TENDING AUTONOMY NEEDS)
- Least clear: *The timing of that first call is important* (OFF RECORD)

As with being pessimistic, apologizing will be more powerful as an acknowledgement of the member's autonomy needs if the leader's apology is authentic rather than conventional. Consider another version of the dialogue used earlier, in Exhibit 10d.

Leader: There's no clear justification for this headache thing. I don't know what the solution might be but don't turn a deaf ear to it.
Member: Yeah. I'm not gonna.
Leader: I'm sorry if I sound like I'm micro-managing, but please differentiate clearly between safety and performance issues.

Exhibit 10d. Example of ON RECORD POLITELY: TENDING AUTONOMY NEEDS: Apologize. (Adapted from Fairhurst & Chandler 1989:239)

In Exhibit 10d, the leader's final contribution tends to the autonomy needs of the member by apologizing for issuing a directive about how the member should perform her task (i.e., *I'm sorry if I sound like I'm micro-managing . . .*). If the leader's apology is sincere, his use of this tactic is more powerful because the leader is truly tending to the autonomy needs of the member by acknowledging that the leader is imposing on the member unfairly. However, if the leader's apology is only conventional, then his use of this tactic is only slightly more polite/less clear than his ON RECORD PLAINLY strategy in Exhibit 7b (i.e., *I suggest you differentiate . . .*).

Be Grateful—Using the seventh and final tactic means being both clear and polite by expressing gratitude or incurring a debt while directing a member.

- Most clear: *Submit your report on Friday* (ON RECORD PLAINLY)
- Moderately clear: *I'd really appreciate getting your report on Friday* (Be Grateful tactic for TENDING AUTONOMY NEEDS)
- Least clear: *It would be helpful to have your report on Friday* (OFF RECORD)

Similarly, you can use this tactic when consulting a member.

- Most clear: *When did the customer first call?* (ON RECORD PLAINLY)
- Moderately clear: *I'll owe you one if you tell me when the customer first called* (Be Grateful tactic for TENDING AUTONOMY NEEDS)
- Least clear: *The timing of that first call is important* (OFF RECORD)

This tactic will be more powerful if the leader is sincere rather than conventional when incurring the debt.

Consider yet another version of the dialogue we've been using, in Exhibit 10e.

Leader: There's no clear justification for this headache thing. I don't know what the solution might be but don't turn a deaf ear to it.
Member: Yeah. I'm not gonna.
Leader: I'll help you deal with HR in any way I can if you clearly differentiate between safety and performance issues.

Exhibit 10e. Example of ON RECORD POLITELY: TENDING AUTONOMY NEEDS: Be Grateful. (Adapted from Fairhurst & Chandler 1989:239)

The leader's final contribution in Exhibit 10c tends to the autonomy needs of the member by offering to help the member if he follows the leader's directive about performing his task (i.e., *I'll help you . . .*). If the leader's offer is authentic, his use of that tactic is more powerful because the leader is truly tending to the autonomy needs of the member by offering the member something of value. As we saw with being pessimistic and apologizing, if the leader's offer is only conventional, then his use of this tactic is only slightly more polite/less clear than his ON RECORD PLAINLY strategy in Exhibit 7b (i.e., *I request you differentiate . . .*).

Before we move on to the question of when TENDING AUTONOMY NEEDS is appropriate, let's return to the memo shown in Exhibit 10a at the beginning of this chapter. The leader went ON RECORD POLITELY by TENDING AUTONOMY NEEDS by using several of the tactics we've covered in this chapter: He impersonalizes his suggestions by addressing *all managers* rather than any individual; he minimizes the imposition of his suggestions by saying *using some of these*; he expresses pessimism about compliance with his suggestions by saying *if all managers would consider*; he apologizes for the imposition at the end of the memo; and he acknowledges his debt by beginning the memo with *I would be grateful*.

When To Use This Strategy

We'll continue our discussion of Exhibit 10a to evaluate the effectiveness of the leader's choice of this strategy. To do so, we must first answer the four questions associated with thinking like a leader:

1. What is the organizational purpose driving you to communicate with the member—and how urgent is your need to act? The leader's goal is to direct organizational members future behavior toward new employees. His goal does not appear to be urgent. (Chapter 2)

2. Is the member part of your in-group? It's likely that a few of the members who will receive this memo are in the leader's in-group. However, the majority are not. (Chapter 3)
3. How will your message affect the member's ego needs? Ego needs are not a salient issue in this situation. (Chapter 4)
4. How will your message affect the member's autonomy needs? Directing the members' behavior threatens their autonomy needs. Interacting with members using the medium of a memo tends their autonomy needs. (Chapter 5)

TENDING AUTONOMY NEEDS is effective in situations in which both your organizational purpose (hence, your intended action) and your rapport with a member are important. As mentioned in Chapter 9, these are probably the most common situations you face as a leader. It appears to describe the situation in Exhibit 10a: The leader wants to influence the behavior of the members, but he wants to mitigate any threat to their autonomy in order to maintain the quality of his relationship with them—especially with those who are not part of his in-group. Thus, the leader's choice of the ON RECORD POLITELY: TENDING AUTONOMY NEEDS strategy is effective in the case of Exhibit 10a.

This strategy is almost always appropriate. However, it will be less effective with members who place little value on autonomy whether because of their readiness in this specific situation or their cultural values in general. Remember that, if your intended action poses no threat to your rapport with the member, you should be using the ON RECORD PLAINLY strategy instead. Let me point out that, because of its efficiency, going ON RECORD PLAINLY is a way of tending to the autonomy needs of members when there is no threat to their autonomy. This will never be the case when *directing* members (since autonomy is at least slightly threatened anytime you communicate this management action). However, it will certainly be true when valuing the member and will sometimes be true when informing or consulting the member.

The Bottom Line: Interacting Like a Leader

The ON RECORD POLITELY: TENDING AUTONOMY NEEDS strategy is accomplished by making your intended actions and meaning clear but polite by using seven tactics:

- Question or Hedge;
- Be Impersonal;
- Minimize;

- Be Deferential;
- Be Pessimistic;
- Apologize;
- Be Grateful.

To manage rapport, you should use this strategy when (a) your organizational purpose is important but threatening to the autonomy needs of the member involved and (b) your relationship with that member is also important.

Further Reading

Brown, P. and Levinson, S. C. (1987) *Politeness: Some Universals in Language Usage. Studies in Interactional Sociolinguistics*, vol. 4. Cambridge: Cambridge University Press.

This book is highly academic, but it is the primary theoretical work upon which the communication strategy we've covered in Chapter 10 is based. The authors call this strategy "negative politeness," and their discussion occurs on pages 129-211.

Applications

10A. Review your answers to Application 5A about the management situation involved in *Courage Under Fire* between the general (played by Michael Moriarty) and colonel (played by Denzel Washington). Remember that the general is under pressure to award the first Medal of Honor to a female military leader but the colonel wants to delay his recommendation because he has received conflicting accounts of the captain's behavior from her subordinates. Their dialogue occurs on a golf course with one of the general's subordinates within hearing distance. What TENDING AUTONOMY NEEDS tactics does the general use? How effective is the general in this management situation? Explain, using specific examples from the dialogue.

General: Submit your report today.
Colonel: Sorry, sir. I won't [sign] an incomplete report.
General: [taking a practice swing] Should I remind who recommended you for this post when no one else would touch you?
Colonel: Are you saying you chose me because I wouldn't rock the boat.
General: Dereliction of duty. . . drunk and disorderly . . . at best dishonorable discharge. . . . I could give you direct orders to submit your report. . . . I handed this to you, Nat—as a way back. You could have had one helluva career. You give Meredith [the colonel's wife] my best. Tell her I didn't have any choice.
Colonel: I'm gonna finish this report—. . . . I'm gonna get this one right. [walking away]

Exhibit 10f. Scene from *Courage Under Fire*.

10B. Consider the scene from the film, *Apollo 13* in Exhibit 10g. The NASA leaders in this situation are confronting the astronaut, Jim Lovell (played by Tom Hanks) with the news that his team member, Ken Mattingly, cannot participate in their upcoming mission because he has contracted the measles. What TENDING AUTONOMY NEEDS tactics do the leaders use to mitigate threats to Lovell's autonomy? How effective are they in this management situation? Explain using specific examples from the dialogue.

Jim Lovell: You wanna break up my crew [right] before the launch . . .
Doctor: Mattingly will be getting seriously ill . . . when you and Hayes will be [rendezvousing] with him.
Deke: Jim, that's a lousy time for a fever.
Jim Lovell: [But] Swigert has been out of the loop for weeks.
Manager at Desk: He's fully qualified to fly.
Jim Lovell: He's a fine pilot. But when was the last time he was in a simulator?
Manager at Desk: I'm sorry, Jim. I understand how you feel. [But] we can either scrub Mattingly and go with Swigert or we can bump all three of you to a later mission.
Deke: Jim, if you hold out for [Mattingly] you will not be on Apollo 13. It's your decision.

Exhibit 10g. Scene from *Apollo 13*.

11
Interacting Like a Leader

To interact like a leader requires that you use your assessment of the management situation (i.e., your answers to the four questions for thinking like a leader) to choose an appropriate strategy for communicating with the member in this situation. There are four possibilities.

A. On Record Plainly. This strategy means being as clear as possible using four tactics:

- Be Explicit and Direct;
- Be First;
- Be Brief;
- Be Organized.

You should use this strategy only when your organizational purpose is of primary importance, whether because your intended action has only positive or neutral effects on your member's needs or because your actions are more important than your relationship with the member. Many management situations will call for this strategy because your actions pose no threat. However, it's crucial to accurately assess effects on members' ego and autonomy needs since you cannot build human commitment to the organization if you habitually privilege the organization's needs over a member's.

B. Off Record. This communication strategy means making your intended actions and meaning ambiguous using three tactics:

- Be Cursory;
- Be Irrelevant;
- Be Figurative.

Although this strategy is more common within highly stratified groups, you should use the Off Record strategy only when your organizational purpose is of little importance. This should be a fairly rare management situation.

C. On Record Politely: Tending Ego Needs. This strategy means making your intended actions and meaning clear but polite by using three tactics:

- Be Positive;
- Be Inclusive;
- Be Present.

You should use this strategy when your message will threaten the member's ego needs; and both your organizational purpose and your relationship with the member are important. Although this strategy is appropriate in many management situations, the Be Positive tactic must be used only with sincerity, and the Be Inclusive tactic only if the member is clearly one of your in-group.

D. On Record Politely: Tending Autonomy Needs. This final strategy means making your intended actions and meaning clear but polite by using seven tactics:

- Question or Hedge;
- Be Impersonal;
- Minimize;
- Be Deferential;
- Be Pessimistic;
- Apologize;
- Be Grateful.

You should use this strategy when your message will threaten the member's autonomy needs; and both your organizational purpose and your relationship with a member are important. Again, this should describe many of the management situations in which you interact with members.

The appropriate use of these four communication strategies for all possible management situations is summarized in Table 11a. Note that the strategies appear in order from most polite/least clear to least polite/most clear.

Management Situation					Recommended Communication Strategy for Managing Rapport
Importance of Manager Action	Importance of Relationship with Member	Message Effects on Rapport: Positive	Message Effects on Rapport: Negative (Autonomy)	Message Effects on Rapport: Negative (Ego)	
–					OFF RECORD
+	+			+	ON RECORD POLITELY by TENDING EGO NEEDS
+	+		+		ON RECORD POLITELY by TENDING AUTONOMY NEEDS
+	–				ON RECORD PLAINLY
+	+	+			ON RECORD PLAINLY

Table 11a. Appropriate use of TILL communication strategies.

Applications

11A. Revisit the annual employee performance evaluation for Doris Johnson (Exhibit 6a) used earlier to test your knowledge of thinking like a leader. Review your answer to Application 6 about the management situation. Your task is to suggest changes to the communication strategies and tactics used by Mr. Russell in three sections of that performance evaluation before they are shared with Doris (reproduced here as Exhibits 11a-c). Refer to Table 11a to identify the most appropriate communication strategies for this situation. Provide suggestions for specific changes and justify each one.

Knowledge, Skills, Abilities – Consider the degree to which the employee exhibits the required level of job knowledge and/or skills to perform the job and this employee's use of established techniques, materials and equipment as they relate to performance.

Unacceptable Superior

☐ 1 ☐ 2 ☒ 3 ☐ 4 ☐ 5

Comments: You have a thorough fundamental knowledge of the guidelines for doing your job. A site visit to Organization Y revealed a great deal of information we were not familiar with. Effort must be made in the verification and filing responsibilities to proactively prevent tremendous backlogs making it difficult to stay current.

Exhibit 11a. Excerpt re: Knowledge, Skills, Abilities from Doris Johnson's performance evaluation.

Work Habits – To what extent does the employee display a positive, cooperative attitude toward work assignments and requirements? Consider compliance with established work rules and organizational policies.

Unacceptable Superior

☐ 1 ☐ 2 ☒ 3 ☐ 4 ☐ 5

Comments: Although your job duties are mostly repetitive, routing processing functions, I can depend on you to report to work and contribute. You uphold the rules we have set for your Area such as requiring individuals to "check out" files and ensure that they are returned. Do not take a defensive stance when constructive criticism is given or your work is evaluated.

Exhibit 11b. Excerpt re: Work Habits from Doris Johnson's performance evaluation.

Judgment – Consider how well the employee effectively analyzes problems, determines appropriate action for solutions, and exhibits timely and decisive action; thinks logically.

Unacceptable Superior

☐ 1 ☒ 2 ☐ 3 ☐ 4 ☐ 5

Comments: We have discussed issues with the underutilization of your part-time aids to get your duties accomplished. Little intervention is needed from me when you encounter issues but some issues could be prevented with proactive measures—getting the Form 3s verified in a timely way to prevent working with an expired document. Do not wait until the situation is at a critical point before informing me. Come to me with recommendations/suggestions not just problems.

Exhibit 11c. Excerpt re: Judgment from Doris Johnson's performance evaluation.

11B. Revisit the dialogue in Exhibit 6b between a manager, John, and his direct report, Pete, used earlier to test your knowledge of thinking like a leader. Review your answer to Application 6B about the management situation. Your task in this application exercise is to identify specific examples of each of the four communication strategies used by the manager, John, and to assess their effectiveness in this situation (see Table 11a).

John: I'd like to talk with you about building personal relationships. My opinion is that many people don't understand you from a business standpoint or a personal standpoint. For some reason, people have this image of you as being very hard core, controlling, and insensitive, and I don't think that's true.
Pete: Yeah.
John: I think that you're real sensitive, but sometimes you're unwilling to share that sensitivity with others. You need to open yourself up to people because it's a lot easier for them to understand that you're caring and that you want to do what's right for the business and for them.
Pete: With the technicians or team leaders, I always look for their suggestions and their input. I rarely make decisions for people. But somehow the work team sees me this way. The first time I realized it was at our off-site. Smith said he saw me as very controlling, very direct. It shocked me. I went home and told my wife, Peg, and she laughed. [John laughs.] So, to me, it's really two different faces.
John: The other data point I have is that some people outside the department made remarks about your controlling behavior. A group manager said, We ought to put Pete in Industrial Relations to soften him up some." [Pete laughs.] So, other people have this hard-core image.
Pete: Well, there's probably some validity.
John: You carry a tremendous load for the module. I know you have a lot of irons in the fire, and you work long and hard. I don't want to tell you to stop doing that, but to some degree you have to in order to establish relationships. I think that you can achieve a better balance. In my first three or four years, I was a lot like you. I thought if I wasn't busy, I wasn't contributing. I got a lot of feedback from secretaries especially. I would go in and say, "Here's what I want. Don't ask me how I'm doing today. Don't give m any of this chit-chat about what the weather's like cause I'm here for business. And that's why you're here, too, by the way."
Pete: [laughs]
John: They told me that I acted like they were the lowest people on the totem pole, and I never intended that. But in the way that I behaved, that's the image that they had of me.
Pete: I think I do that with the work team. I guess that's what I'm hearing. silence]

Exhibit 11d. Leader-member interaction.
(Adapted from Fairhurst & Sarr 1996:104, 118.)

12
Conclusion

TILL provides an emotionally intelligent system for describing how to think and interact like a leader. Figure 12a summarizes what it takes. Starting at the top of the figure, you must understand your **organizational goals** (e.g. maximizing output) and the specific **management actions** derived from those goals (e.g. directing a member of your organization to improve his or her performance). You must also understand what is influencing your strategy for communicating that action (like the **urgency** of an upcoming meeting). Perhaps most importantly, you must accurately assess the quality of your relationship with the member as well as the likely effect of your action on that relationship (**rapport**) based on your member's ego and autonomy needs. At this point, you have accurately assessed the management situation you face.

To interact like a leader, you must use your assessment of the situation to choose one of four strategies for communicating with the member. These strategies enable you to manage **rapport effects**: (1) ON RECORD PLAINLY when your organizational purpose is of primary importance, whether because your intended action has only positive or neutral effects on your rapport with the member or because your actions are more important than that rapport; (2) OFF RECORD when your organizational purpose is unimportant; (3) ON RECORD POLITELY: TENDING EGO NEEDS when both your purpose and relationship are important and the member's ego needs are threatened; or ON RECORD POLITELY: TENDING AUTONOMY NEEDS when both your purpose and relationship are important and the member's autonomy needs are threatened.

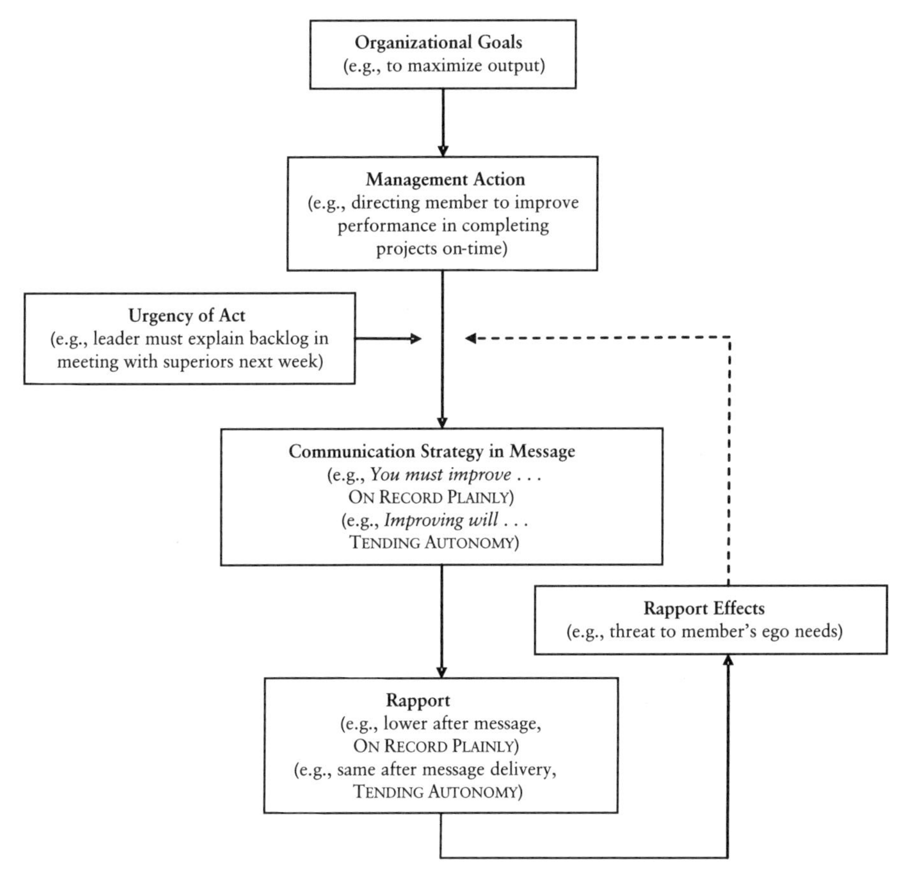

Figure 12a. Model of the TILL system for effective interpersonal communication.

TILLing Two Leaders

Let's return to the dialogue from *Crimson Tide* in which we compared two leaders in two scenes interacting with members. We will examine each scene in detail to demonstrate how the TILL system predicts the quality of leader-member relations.

The first interaction involves a leader named Hunter who has just witnessed a fight on the ship between two male subordinates and is interacting with one of them named Rivetti. Their conversation is analyzed in Exhibit 12a.

Begins with consulting member rather than directing or informing. (*On Record Plainly*)	**Hunter:** Rivetti, what's up?
	Rivetti: Sorry, sir. Just a difference of opinion that got out of hand.
Repeats question. (*On Record Plainly*)	**Hunter:** What about?
	Rivetti: . . . I'd rather just forget about it. [Sir]
Refuses member's attempt to avoid answering. (*On Record Plainly*)	**Hunter:** I don't [care] what you'd rather forget about.
	Rivetti: [pause] Well, I said the Kirby silver surfer was the only real silver surfer. And that the Mobius silver surfer was shit. And Benefield's a big Mobius fan. And uh things got out of hand. . . .
Informs member of role expectations. Tends to member's quality and social role face wants. (*On Record Plainly*)	**Hunter:** Rivetti, you're a supervisor. You can get a commission . . .
	Rivetti: . . . It'll never happen again, [Sir].
Directs member's future behavior. Informs member of consequences for noncompliance. (*On Record Plainly*)	**Hunter:** It better not . . . . I see this kind of nonsense I'm gonna write you up. You understand?
	Rivetti: Yes, sir.
Ends by tending to the relationship. (*Off Record*)	**Hunter:** You have to set an example even in the face of stupidity. . . . Everybody who reads comic books knows . . . Kirby silver surfer is the only real silver surfer. . . . am I right or wrong?
	Rivetti: [laughing] You're right, sir.

Exhibit 12a. A TILL analysis of interaction between a leader (Executive Officer Hunter) and organizational member (Seaman Rivetti) in *Crimson Tide*.

Using TILL, we can describe several reasons why Hunter is perceived as an effective leader on the basis of his interaction with Rivetti. First, he begins the interaction by consulting rather than directing or informing (*What's up?*). In other words, he begins the interaction with a leadership rather than a management message.

Second, Hunter primarily uses On Record Plainly communication tactics with Rivetti. He makes his intended action explicit when consulting by using interrogatives (e.g., *what's up?*) and when warning Rivetti (e.g., *I'm gonna write you up*). In addition, Hunter gives only needed information when informing Rivetti of his role expectations (e.g., *you're a supervisor*). Thus, his management message is very clear because of his use of the Be Explicit and Be Brief tactics.

Third, Hunter's actions within this interchange involve all four quadrants of the COMPETING VALUES FRAMEWORK (Figure 2a): He not only consults, informs, and directs Rivetti, but also focuses on his relationship with Rivetti. He tends to the member's ego needs by using Rivetti's name and second person pronouns (e.g., *you're a supervisor*) and agreeing with him (e.g., *Kirby silver surfer is the only real silver surfer*). Thus, Hunter actively manages rapport through his use of TENDING EGO NEEDS tactics.

Fourth, note that when Hunter's intended action is primarily about valuing Rivetti, he uses OFF RECORD tactics like being cursory and irrelevant (e.g., *Everybody who reads comic books knows*)—his intended act is unstated and has nothing to do with comic books. As we noted earlier, the choice of an OFF RECORD strategy for building relationships is the most common among men, especially in a military culture where more direct expressions are discouraged (Tannen 1994). Finally, Hunter ends the interaction with a leadership message focused on personal interests rather than a management message focused on professional interests. In sum, Hunter's communication strategy emphasizes both tasks and relationships.

Now let's compare the interaction in Exhibit 12a with another that occurs just a few minutes later in the same film involving the leader, Captain Ramsey, and his male subordinates, including Hunter. Their interchange is analyzed in Exhibit 12b.

Informs Hunter of his opinion. (*On Record Plainly*)	**Ramsey:** Feels like the whole crew needs a kick in the ass. **Hunter:** Or a pat on the back, sir. [pause] I just witnessed a fight down in crew's mess. . . . I think the men are uh a bit on edge . . . . Morale seems to be a bit low.
Discounts Hunter's opinion (*OFF RECORD*) or Agrees with Hunter (*On Record Plainly*)	**Ramsey:** [smirking while making eye contact with Hunter] Well, you seem to have the pulse of the men . . . . [communicating over intercom to ship's crew] May I have your attention please. [pause] Mr. Hunter has brought it to my attention that morale may be a bit low.
Directs members' future behavior. (*OFF RECORD*) Informs members of current situation. (*On Record Plainly*)	**Ramsey:** [pauses while looking at Hunter] So I suggest this. Any crew member who feels he can't handle the situation can leave the ship right now. [pause] Gentleman, war is imminent. [pause] This is the captain. [pause] That is all. **Hunter:** Very inspiring, sir.

Exhibit 12b. A TILL analysis of interaction between a leader (Captain Ramsey) and organizational members (including Executive Officer Hunter) in *Crimson Tide*.

Using TILL, we can describe several reasons why Ramsey is usually perceived as a less effective leader than Hunter. First, Ramsey's actions fall exclusively in the lower half of the COMPETING VALUES FRAMEWORK, making his sole focus a management rather than leadership message.

Second, when Ramsey addresses Hunter's comment about morale by saying, *you seem to have the pulse of the men*, he uses sarcasm to discount Hunter's opinion. Because of his use of the OFF RECORD strategy, Ramsey's meaning is ambiguous, and Hunter responds as if Ramsey goes ON RECORD PLAINLY with a compliment.

Third, Ramsey directs the members' future behavior by discounting their mental state and uses irony again (*Any crew member who feels he can't handle the situation can leave the ship right now*): Because Ramsey's suggestion cannot be followed while they are in the middle of the ocean, his meaning is less ambiguous but still OFF RECORD.

Finally, Ramsey ends by informing members of their current situation by going ON RECORD PLAINLY, which effectively ignores their ego needs (i.e., Hunter suggests they need a pat on the back).

In sum, Hunter promotes organizational goals by clearly informing and directing Rivetti but also promotes trust and commitment by accurately predicting the threats to rapport inherent in his actions. Thus, Hunter tends to the leader-member relationship in an emotionally intelligent way by managing rapport through his choice of interpersonal communication strategies designed to tend the member's needs. In contrast, Ramsey promotes organizational goals by sarcastically (and ambiguously) informing and directing members and does nothing to satisfy his members' needs. Hunter uses both position power and personal power to lead, while Ramsey relies solely on his position power (French & Raven 1959). The TILL system of effective leadership communication introduced in this book is designed to help you increase your own personal power.

The Bottom Line: Thinking and Interacting Like a Leader

I have presented leadership as one component of management: While managers focus on organizational tasks, leaders focus on organizational relationships. I began this book by pointing out the importance of communication satisfaction in successful organizations—leaders must be expert communicators in order to build better relationships with members and influence communication satisfaction (as well as productivity, job satisfaction and performance, and organizational effectiveness). Unfortunately, most leaders do not have the needed skills—what's worse—they don't recognize they lack them.

Within the COMPETING VALUES FRAMEWORK, we saw that managers become more effective not only by informing and directing members but also by valuing and consulting with them. This focus on relationships is what makes leaders out of managers. The TILL system is different from most approaches to leadership communication precisely because it focuses on the ability to manage relationships by thinking like a leader about management situations: You know the purpose of your intended interaction with a member, its urgency, and your current rapport with that member, along with the potential effect of your action on your future rapport with that member. Interacting like a leader means using that knowledge to choose one of four communication strategies which vary along the clarity/politeness continuum.

There are no short cuts to stimulating growth of successful relationships. If you have worked your way through the chapters in this book (as well as the applications) you know that, while using the TILL system is time-consuming in the beginning, it provides a pattern for thinking and interacting that works and becomes habitual with practice.

Applications

12A. Read through the scene in Exhibit 12a from the film *Norma Rae*. Norma begins by addressing a volunteer named Peter who arrives for his union duties late. Your task is to assess whether Rubin, a union organizer, was interacting like a leader with Norma by identifying the management situation he faced and the communication strategies he chose for his messages. You should refer to Table 11a to gauge the effectiveness of Rubin's communication strategies for this management situation. You should assume that Norma is part of Rubin's in-group before this interaction. Point to specific examples to support your assessment.

Norma Rae: You're supposed to be here at 3:15. It's 4:15. . . . You working for this union or aren't ya?
Peter: I was getting my tooth filled.
Norma Rae: You were getting your beer gut filled.
Peter: Get off me, Norma.
Norma Rae: I'm just startin in on you. [She continues chewing him out.]
Rubin: Norma, shut your cake hole. . . [walking toward her] Now get the hell outta the office.
Norma Rae: I only said what was true.
Rubin: Out. . . [Norma leaves] Peter, get to work. [A few minutes later, Rubin enters the restaurant where Norma has gone and sits next to her]
Rubin: Mouthy. . . you're too muscular. You can't come down that hard on a man and leave him his balls. Easy. . . .
Norma Rae: You're right. I've got a big mouth.
Rubin: Uh huh.
Norma Rae: You know cotton mill workers is known as trash to some. I know the union's the only way we're gonna get our own voice. . . . I guess that's why I push. [Rubin begins eating the pie sitting in front of Norma, which she has not touched]
Rubin: Our own Mother Jones . . . . If the situation ever called for a smart, loud, profane, sloppy, hard-workin' woman, I'd pick you every time, kid.
Norma Rae: How come sloppy?

Exhibit 12c. Scene from *Norma Rae*.

12B. Read the scene in Exhibit 12d from *The Bounty*. The crew of a ship has recently sailed from England in 1787 with their captain, William Bligh (played by Anthony Hopkins in this 1984 film) and executive officer John Fryer (played by Daniel Day-Lewis). This interaction takes place during their attempt to sail around Cape Horn during a very dangerous storm.

Fryer: We should turn back.
Bligh: What?
Fryer: In my opinion, we should put about.
Bligh: In my opinion, we should not, sir. We keep on going.
Fryer: We'll never make it around the Horn. We MUST turn back!. . . . I want my opinion in the log, [Sir].
Bligh: Very well, Mr. Fryer. You'll get what you wish.
Fryer: The ship can't stand it!
Bligh: The ship can stand it very well.
Fryer: And how long do you think the men can stand it?
Bligh: As long as the officers can, Mr. Fryer.

Exhibit 12d. Scene from *The Bounty*.

Your task is to assess whether Bligh was interacting like a leader by identifying the management situation he faced and the communication strategies he chose for his messages. You should refer to Table 11a to gauge the effectiveness of his communication strategies for this management situation.

Now compare the following dialogue in Exhibit 12e that takes place when Bligh addresses the officers and crew after surviving the storm by giving up the attempt to sail around Cape Horn. He begins by announcing that he is replacing Mr. Fryer with Mr. Christian, as second in command.

Fryer: [heads for the door in disbelief]
Bligh: Mr. Fryer, come back here. [Fryer keeps walking] Mr. Fryer, sir, COME IN HERE! [Fryer turns and moves back near Bligh]
Fryer: This is an outrage.
Bligh: Mr. Fryer . . .
Fryer: [interrupting] In all my years at sea . . .
Bligh: [interrupting] Your years at sea! Good lord, man, if I'd known your nature, I would not have accepted you as bosun of a river barge.
Fryer: Must I suffer this in front of the men?
Bligh: You'll suffer my correction wherever you're at fault, sir!
Fryer: [raising voice] WHAT fault, sir?
Bligh: [screaming] God damn it, man, you turned your back on me!!
Fryer: And for that I apologize.
Bligh: Very well . . .
Fryer: But I protest . . .
Bligh: [interrupting] You protest, do you?
Fryer: I am master of the boat.
Bligh: [screaming even more loudly] And I say I am COMMANDER. By law. . . . DO YOU UNDERSTAND!!

Exhibit 12e. More interaction from *The Bounty*.

Your task is to assess whether Bligh was interacting like a leader by identifying the management situation he faced and the communication strategies he chose for his messages. Refer again to Table 11a to gauge the effectiveness of his communication strategies for this management situation. Finally, compare the effectiveness of Bligh in thinking and interacting like a leader in the two management situations.

References

Brown, P. and Levinson, S. A. 1987. *Politeness: Some universals in language usage. Studies in interactional sociolinguistics.* Cambridge: Cambridge University Press.

Campbell, K. S., White, C. D., and Johnson, D. 2003. Leader-member relations as a function of rapport management. *Journal of Business Communication*, 40, 170–194.

Daft, R. L. and Lengel, R. H. 1986. Organizational information requirements, media richness and structural design. *Management Science, 32*, 554–571.

Delahoussaye, M. 2001. Leadership in the 21st century. Part One. *Training*, August, 50–59.

Delahoussaye, M. 2001. Leadership in the 21st century. Part Two. *Training*, September, 60–72.

Donnellon, A. 1996. *Team talk: The power of language in team dynamics.* Boston: Harvard Business School Press.

Fairhurst, G. T. and Chandler, T. A. 1989. Social structure in leader-member interaction. *Communication Monographs, 56*, 215–239.

Fairhurst, G. T. and Sarr, R. A. 1996. *The art of framing: Managing the language of leadership*. San Francisco: Jossey-Bass.

French, J. R. P. and Raven, B. 1959. The bases of social power. In D. Cartwright (ed.), *Studies in social power.* Ann Arbor: University of Michigan Press, 219–236.

Goffman, E. 1967. *Interaction ritual: Essays on face-to-face behavior.* Garden City, NY: Random House.

Goleman, D., Boyatzis, R. and McKee, A. 2002. *Primal leadership: Realizing the power of emotional intelligence.* Boston: Harvard Business School Press.

Graen, G. B. and Cashman, J. F. 1975. A role-making of leadership in formal organizations: A developmental approach. In J. G. Hunt and L. L. Larson (eds.) *Leadership frontiers.* Kent, OH: Kent State University Press, 143–165.

Graen, G. B. and Scandura, T. 1987. Toward a psychology of dyadic organizing. *Research in Organizational Behavior, 9*, 175–208.

Grice, H. P. 1975. Logic and conversation. In P. Cole and J. L. Morgan (eds.) *Syntax and semantics 3: Speech acts*. New York: Academic Press, 41–58.

Hackman, M. Z. and Johnson, C. E. 2003. *Leadership: A communication perspective*, 4th ed. Prospect Heights, IL: Waveland Press.

Hammer, R. 1990. *The Helmsleys: The rise and fall of Harry and Leona.* London: Penguin.

Hargie, O. and Tourish, D. 2000. *Handbook of communication audits for organisations*. London: Routledge.
Hersey, P. and Blanchard, K. H. 1988. *Management of organizational behavior: Utilizing human resources*. Englewood Cliffs, NJ: Prentice Hall.
Hofstede, G. 2001. *Culture's consequences: Comparing values, behaviors, institutions, and organizations across nations*. Thousand Oaks, CA: Sage.
Kellerman, B. 2004. *Bad leadership: What it is. How it happens. Why it matters*. Boston: Harvard Business School Press.
McKirchy, K. 1998. *Powerful performance appraisals: How to set expectations and work together to improve performance*. Franklin Lakes, NJ: Career Press.
Miller, L. 2000. Negative assessments in Japanese-American workplace interaction. In H. Spencer-Oatey (ed.), *Culturally speaking: Managing rapport through talk across cultures*. London: Continuum, 240–254.
Mintzberg, H. 1975. The manager's job: Folklore and fact. *Harvard Business Review*, July-August, 49–61.
Nelson, B. 2003. What do employees want? *ABA Bank Marketing*, March: 9.
Quinn, R.E. 1991. *Beyond rational management: Mastering the paradoxes and competing demands of high performance*. San Francisco: Jossey-Bass.
Searle, J. 1976. The classification of illocutionary acts. *Language in Society, 5*, 1–24.
Soder, R. 2001. *The language of leadership*. San Francisco: Jossey-Bass.
Spencer-Oatey, H. 2000. Rapport management: A framework for analysis. In H. Spencer-Oatey (ed.), *Culturally speaking: Managing rapport through talk across cultures*. London: Continuum, 11–46.
Tannen, D. 1994. *Talking from 9 to 5/ Women and men in the workplace: Language, sex, and power*. New York: Avon.
Watson Wyatt. 2005. Connecting organizational communication to financial performance: 2003/2004 communication ROI study. Washington, DC. Available on 7/20/05 at http://www.watsonwyatt.com/research/resrender.asp?id=w-698&page=1.
White, C. D. 2005. Development and validation of a measure of leader rapport management behavior. Paper presented at Academy of Management, August 10, 2005, Oahu, Hawaii.

Answers to Selected Application Exercises

This section of the book provides you with possible answers to the Application A exercises from the end of each chapter. While these samples are not the only "correct" answers, they do represent "good" ones in that they demonstrate an understanding of the content in each chapter as applied to a novel management situation.

Application 1A

Categorizing the Foreman's and Juror #8's behaviors might look something like this:

Leadership Theory or Model from Table 1a	Jury Foreman	Juror #8
Michigan Leadership Studies	Interested in output	Interested in individuality and personal needs
Ohio State Leadership Studies	Goal-achievement oriented	Respectful
McGregor's Theory X	?	Self-control
Tannenbaum-Schmidt Continuum	Position-based power; democratic	Motivation
Fiedler's Contingency Theory	Clear procedures; cooperation	Cooperation

The Foreman's behavior is categorized as predominantly task-oriented despite a limited relationship-focus (e.g., democratic and cooperation). More specifically, the Foreman appears to focus on task efficiency from beginning to end of this interaction. Thus, it seems more accurate to call him a "manager" or "bureaucrat" than a "leader." He immediately said, *you gentlemen can handle this any way you want to . . . If we want to discuss it first and then vote, that's one way. Or we can vote right now and see how we stand.* If he had been concerned with the effectiveness of the jury, as opposed to their efficiency, he would have reviewed some of the issues in detail and then promoted discussion by consulting members about their opinions. It appeared that he only wanted to get to the end of their task, a unanimous vote, without regard for the quality of that vote. The comments he made throughout exemplified his task-orientation because he focused only on getting the members of the jury back on task (e.g., *we have a job to do. Let's do it*).

Juror #8's "not guilty" vote could be seen as task-oriented behavior. It dictated that the group would have to discuss their opinions. He seemed more interested in the quality of their voting task and on the person who would be most affected by that vote—the accused. Unlike the Foreman, Juror #8 focused on people as well as their task. That relationship focus, as shown by the categorization of his behaviors on the previous page, made him more of a "leader" than the Foreman. Instead of simply telling the others what he thought (or what they should think), he stated his uncertainty (e.g., *I don't know whether I believe it or not*) and asked questions for the others to consider (e.g., *Are we to vote on his face?*); he invited them to join in a discussion of the issues. In addition, Juror #8 displayed a great deal of self-control, treating others with respect when it would have been easy to respond to those who attacked him with derogatory remarks (e.g., *You're in left field*).

Application 2A

It seems as if the primary goal of the letter is to consolidate organizational processes by informing external members (Volunteer Editors) of changes being made to internal and external systems at the organization. If the point of the letter is to inform, it does an admirable job. It provides the audience with quite a bit of information regarding changes which are being made to both internal and external systems, although you are not really sure of the necessity of some of the information for the audience.

When viewed from the context of an apology letter (which would build commitment by valuing the members), the effect is very poor. The first sentence makes the informational goal seem most important (i.e., *I am writing to you to give you an update on the status of our journal schedules*), while the apology does not occur until the last few sentences of the message. The most glaring problem with the letter in the context of an apology is the distinction made in dealing with the larger problem of the internal staff and the less pressing issues dealing with the external staff. The internal staff, responsible for 64% of the delays, and the group for whom Frank is responsible, is basically defended for their poor performance. The leader makes excuses for the delays associated with the internal staff—from the steep learning curve associated with the new editing/composition system to the unexpected number of staff who had to be replaced.

Managers must actively pursue a greater level of human impact for true leadership to occur. If the ultimate goal is to elicit change in business systems—if a manager ignores emotional impact (no matter what the reason), then the only goal the manager will be successful in achieving is alienation. And if employees ultimately are responsible for the operations of those systems, alienating those very employees seems like bad business. If you are in the business of managing, for effective leadership to occur, employee needs (emotion) can't take second priority to managing systems. Leaders must demonstrate emotional intelligence.

So, I do think the letter was very informative, but if most employees/volunteers in the organization ignored the information because they felt alienated and angry then all the information was wasted and the memo clearly was not effective.

Application 3A

It was easy to tell who was in the ultimate out-group—the doctor who was shown the door before the meeting started!

Because in-group members and leaders exchange more information, one way to determine members of the in-group in this situation is to examine what the leader and members knew when they sat down at the table.

Officer Borodin seems to be the "most" in-group member. He definitely knew about the defection and the murder. In addition, he was the one who asked the doctor to leave, sat next to the captain, and reminded Officer Slavin that he was not captain (i.e., Borodin spoke for or defended the Captain). Finally, he was the only person that Captain Ramius communicated with at the beginning of the scene.

All of the other officers were less in-group than Borodin but more in-group than the doctor. They knew about the defection but not the murder. Out of all the other officers, Chief Engineer Slavin openly confronted the captain. That could mean he was more of an in-group member. His willingness to confront the captain led me to believe that their relationship was firm enough that it could withstand this confrontation (even if the captain was angry or unresponsive). Slavin was also one of the few who seemed to take the murder in stride, going so far as to even say he didn't care about the murder but was upset that the decision was not made by the group. This suggests that he, along with the rest of the in-group, was consulted about other decisions.

Aside from the doctor, I don't think any of the officers were in the out-group or else they wouldn't have been at the table during this meeting. But the ones who seemed to be shocked at the murder and the one who suggested they go back could be more out-group. The captain was the ultimate member of the in-group since he alone decided to send the defection letter to the admiral. This analysis is depicted graphically in the following table.

Who Knew What

Leader/member	Red October Defection	Murder of Party Officer	Letter to Admiral
Captain Ramius	Yes	Yes	Yes
Officer Borodin	Yes	Yes	No
Other Officers	Yes	No	No
Doctor	No	No	No

Application 4A

Mr. Turkel and Mr. Lutz appear to be informing Tess about the status of her application and expressing the value they place on her by offering her a potential promotion through a manager in a different department or division of the organization named Bob Speck. Unfortunately, if you've seen this movie, you know that when Tess meets with Bob, his only interest in her is personal rather than professional. Even if you haven't seen the movie, you can guess that something "stinks" when the suggestion is that Tess meet Bob for a drink and then she responds by saying, *This isn't another set up?* and Mr. Lutz says, *Do I look like a pimp?* It's possible to interpret Tess' question as a threat to Mr. Lutz's ego needs.

More importantly, however, her managers are willing to tend her ego needs related to being a potential date (that's the less cynical way to describe how they see her assets) but threaten her ego needs related to being a potential professional peer. Mr. Turkel devalues Tess' education (*What do you got? Some night school, some secretarial time on your sheet?*).

Application 5A

The general's focus is on directing the colonel to complete the report immediately in order to maximize organizational output. It appears more likely that the leader is trying to take advantage of trust and commitment in this situation rather than to maintain or enhance the colonel's current level of trust and commitment (e.g., *Should I remind you who recommended you for this post when no one else would touch you?*).

The colonel's autonomy needs are definitely threatened because his leader tells him what to do and when in no uncertain terms (i.e., *Submit your report today*). The one instance when the general tends to the colonel's autonomy rights is when he says *I could give you direct orders to submit your report.*

Near the end of the interaction, the leader allows the colonel to choose for himself whether or not he will complete the report as requested.

The entire situation is caused by the colonel demanding his autonomy rights in completing the report under his own terms. At the end of the interaction, the colonel threatens the leader's autonomy rights by saying *I'm gonna finish this report—on my own if I have to.*

Application 6A

Mr. Russell focuses mostly on the lower left quadrant of the competing values model by informing Doris. There is less focus on actually directing her in a way that would maximize her output, and even less on valuing her in order to built trust and commitment. There is little evidence that Mr. Russell has consulted Doris about the content of this performance review. Although the leader indicates that they have had monthly meetings for the last year, he states that she is not keeping him informed on a regular basis. Thus, I believe the leader's overriding organizational purpose in this performance review is to consolidate organizational processes by informing the member of his assessment of her past performance.

Although a performance review can benefit all parties involved, the very nature of an evaluation is a threatening prospect to employees regardless of their actual performance. This particular review is likely to be seen by Doris as severely threatening.

The vast majority of Mr. Russell's comments, as well as his performance ratings, threaten Doris' ego needs (e.g., *Effort must be made in the verification and filing responsibilities to proactively prevent tremendous backlogs* and *We consistently maintain a backlog of incomplete Form 3s, which indicates we are out of compliance with regulations. This was noted on last year's evaluation with an expectation for improvement*). Although the leader makes some attempts to tend to Doris' ego needs (e.g., *I can depend on you to report to work and contribute*), he undermines nearly every attempt by threatening the member's ego needs right before or after (e.g., *your job duties are mostly repetitive* or *Do not take a defensive stance when constructive criticism is given*).

Several statements indicate that Mr. Russell has tended Doris' autonomy needs in the past (e.g., *Little intervention is needed from me when you encounter issues* and *I have consistently encouraged you to identify ideas on changing the process to make it attainable*). The one statement that really intrigues me is *I will work with you on evaluating suggestions of ideas but I will not, nor could not, be responsible for making these.* I think that, while the leader tends to the member's autonomy needs, he appears to ignore her ego needs by withholding the help she may need.

There is no doubt that this performance review will weaken an already poor leader-member relationship. Doris' status as an out-group member is solidified after receiving this evaluation. She has been in this position for 5 years, and I suspect that she will not be there much longer. I also suspect that communication between the leader and member has been getting worse to the point that Doris does not want to interact with her manager at all. The relationship will not get better as a result of this evaluation, nor do I think that Doris will try to substantially improve her performance. In conclusion, Mr. Russell acts more as a manager with limited emotional intelligence than as a leader in this management situation.

Application 7A

Ms. Parker appears to have two organizational purposes for writing this letter: to consolidate internal processes related to financial record-keeping within the organization and to maximize output related to the way Ms. Kwon completes record-keeping in the future. Thus, the manager's primary actions are informing and directing Ms. Kwon.

Ms. Parker definitely signals that her organizational purpose is the primary concern. She makes her actions explicit by using the words *inform* and *warning* when describing the purpose of the letter (*this letter is to inform you . . .* and *this is a written warning . . .*). In addition, the writer places her statement about the informational purpose of the letter as the first sentence of the letter (Be First tactic). However, her statement about her directive purpose appears as the last sentence. Finally, the manager provides only needed information (Be Brief tactic) by making the letter relatively short. The only detail describes the aspects of record-keeping that are the focus of the warning (e.g., *the counter releases were not uploaded for October . . .*) and the organizational consequences (e.g., *these mistakes caused a tremendous burden of time and effort . . .*). In addition, Ms. Parker is concise when she threatens the ego needs of Ms. Kwon (e.g., *this is unacceptable* and *these types of mistakes won't be tolerated in the future*). Similarly, the repetition of the word *mistakes* makes the manager's meaning plain.

In contrast, Ms. Parker includes only one comment that signals any relationship focus in this letter (*although you were not responsible for the upload at these times . . .*). Thus, Ms. Parker functions mostly as a manager in this situation because she focuses on the lower half of the competing values model and on tasks rather than people. This is likely to be effective in this management situation because the record-keeping mistakes could not be tolerated. Ms. Kwon could not misunderstand the seriousness of those mistakes nor the future consequences, after this letter.

Application 8A

While Nakada is attempting to inform Ember that the ad copy won't be used, Ember is attempting to persuade Nakada that it should be. Rapport between the co-workers is threatened because Nakada must not only disagree with Ember's opinion but reject the copy he wrote for the ad they are discussing. This will threaten Ember's ego needs.

Nakada's question (I*s that so?*) and positive comment about the ad copy (*The idea is very clear to me now*) are irrelevant (OFF RECORD) to his purpose of informing Ember the ad copy had been rejected. The closest Nakada gets to mentioning the rejection is when he makes a negative comment about the copy (*But too much pitch for the visual*). This is certainly a cursory means (OFF RECORD) of conveying the rejection. Nakada's use of *maybe* and *yeah* are either irrelevant or cursory statements about the rejection. Finally, because of the cultural and linguistic differences between the co-workers, Ember is likely to misinterpret Nakada's comment, *Let's think about it*, which is a ritualized way of rejecting an idea in Japanese.

Being cursory and irrelevant might work with a native Japanese speaker who could better "read" between the lines. Unless Ember is far more fluent in Japanese culture than I am, I don't see how he could possibly know that the ad copy has been rejected after talking with Nakada. Thus, Nakada avoided threatening Ember's face needs, but I would have to argue that Nakada's use of the OFF RECORD strategy is ineffective in this situation. When Ember eventually learns that his ad copy isn't used, he will feel confused and probably betrayed. Nakada will have undermined Ember's trust rather than protected his ego needs.

Application 9A

Mr. Holland's main purpose in both situations seems to be to maximize output. In other words, he is trying to improve his students' performance in his class on music theory. In both situations, the teacher's primary actions are informing and directing the students, but in the second situation he also does some consulting and valuing. Leader-member rapport is threatened in each situation because of Mr. Holland's criticism of the students' performance, which threatens the students' ego needs. But he only aggravates that threat in the first interaction (Exhibit 10f), while he mitigates it in the second (Exhibit 10g). I believe he acts more as a manager of performance in the first interaction and more as a leader of performance in the second.

Mr. Holland handles poor performance in Exhibit 10f in the worst possible way—he publicly humiliates his students. He personalizes instead of impersonalizes the poor performance of two students in this interaction (*Ms. Swedland, your answer was . . .* and *Mr. Mims your answer was . . .*). This makes his message more plain than his initial statement that was impersonal (*these tests are pathetic*)—TENDING AUTONOMY NEEDS. In addition, he goes OFF RECORD by using sarcasm when he says *this is my favorite*. Finally, when he kicks Mr. Sullivan out of his classroom during the class meeting, he performs the ultimate ego and autonomy threat using the ON RECORD PLAINLY strategy (*get your books and get OUT of here!*). In his final statements during this interaction, Mr. Holland goes ON RECORD PLAINLY in explicitly directing the remaining students' behavior by using the imperative: *get your textbooks out*. Mr. Holland threatens both ego and autonomy needs of his students throughout this interaction. There is no attention to people, only tasks.

In the interaction in Exhibit 10g, Mr. Holland is also addressing the poor performance of his students, but he also admits his responsibility for that performance when he says *I just wanted to confirm that I've made absolutely no impact on you*. Although he minimizes his statement slightly by using *just* (ON RECORD POLITELY), his admission is still clear by using the first person pronoun *I* and saying *absolutely no impact*. At that point in the interaction, Mr. Holland begins mitigating the threat to his students by using the TENDING EGO NEEDS strategy. He moves out of the lower or transactional half of the competing values model and begins consulting the students in an authentic way about their music preferences. He appears to listen, uses in-group markers by focusing on music the students said they like, and signals the value of the individual students by using their names in a positive rather than negative situation. In addition, Mr. Holland signals the in-group status of most of the class by teasing the student who says he listens to classical music. Although the students' poor performance is still the underlying reason for the interaction, Mr. Holland mitigates the ego threats by listening and doing more to make them feel like part of the in-group, and he mitigates autonomy threats by allowing the students to learn about music theory using music that meets their standards for quality instead of his own.

Application 10A

The general's goal is primarily to direct the colonel to complete the report immediately (i.e., to maximize organizational output). The entire situation is caused by the colonel demanding his autonomy needs in completing the report on his own terms. However, the colonel's autonomy needs are threatened because his leader tells him what to do and when, in no uncertain terms. Furthermore, the colonel's ego needs are threatened a number of times by the leader when he mentions the colonel's past transgressions. To make those threats even more offensive, they occur in front of a bystander.

The general does little to mitigate the rapport effects in this situation. However, he does use the ON RECORD POLITELY: TENDING AUTONOMY NEEDS strategy several times. For instance, he uses the interrogative *should I remind you who recommended you for this post when no one else would touch you?* instead of saying *I want to remind you . . .* As discussed in our reading, however, the general's use of this tactic in this situation appears to be conventional rather than authentic—which does little to mitigate the threat to the colonel. Most importantly, there seems to be little organizational purpose behind reminding the colonel of the general's past support; instead, the general appears to be expressing his own feelings of frustration and disappointment. The one instance when the general tends to the colonel's autonomy needs in an authentic way is when he says *I could give you direct orders to submit your report* (the Be Pessimistic tactic).

The general also uses the ON RECORD POLITELY: TENDING EGO NEEDS strategy near the end of the interaction. More specifically, the leader mentions the colonel's wife as a way of indicating the member's in-group status (i.e., *you give Meredith my best. Tell her I didn't have any choice*). Unfortunately, all of the general's ego-threatening statements up to this point in the interaction couldn't be nullified (e.g., his listing of past transgressions and *you could have had one helluva career*).

This was a tough management situation for the general because it was impossible for him to "win." If he supported the colonel's autonomy needs by sanctioning the delay for submitting the recommendation report, it would have negative organizational consequences as well as negative career consequences for the colonel. On the other hand, if he ignored the colonel's autonomy needs and ordered the report to be submitted, it would have effectively dissolved any rapport left between him and the member. Nevertheless, the general might have better managed rapport in this situation by (a) remaining silent about his own feelings or stating them with a more direct communication strategy (e.g., *I am frustrated and disappointed, Nat*) and (b) not voicing the ego-threatening statements about the colonel's past problems.

Application 11A

The current version of Doris' performance evaluation is very clearly task-focused. To repeat from Exercise 6, Mr. Russell focuses mostly on the lower left quadrant of the competing values model by informing Doris. There is less focus on actually directing her in a way that would maximize her output, and even less on valuing her in order to built trust and commitment. There is little evidence that Mr. Russell has consulted Doris about the content of this performance review. Although the leader indicates that they have had monthly meetings for the last year, he states that she is not keeping him informed on a regular basis. Thus, I believe the leader's overriding organizational purpose in this performance review is to consolidate organizational processes by informing the member of his assessment of her past performance. It seems as if his own emotions (frustration, disappointment, etc.) limit his ability to interact with Doris in an emotionally intelligent way.

If Mr. Russell's ratings are "accurate," the leader faces a situation in which the management action (and message) is clearly important but so is the leader's relationship with Doris. Thus, the evaluation needs to have a greater focus on Doris' needs in order to demonstrate Mr. Russell's ability to interact like a leader.

My analysis is summarized in Table 11b. The section of the performance evaluation reproduced in Exhibit 11a is actually the first section of the report. Mr. Russell begins with a positive comment (*you have a thorough fundamental knowledge of...*), but he ends that section with the directive statement about Form 3s shown in Table 11b. Because the leader directs Doris' behavior related to Form 3s in at least one other place in the evaluation, it seems wiser for him to go OFF RECORD with the directive in this beginning section of the report, privileging his relationship with the member over his organization goal. In this way, his praise would make more of an impact. If Mr. Russell feels his organizational goal must appear in this initial section of the evaluation, then I would recommend he go ON RECORD PLAINLY with it as I've indicated above. In other words, I would prefer to see the leader take a stand at beginning of the evaluation.

Section of Report	Management Action & Original Strategy (tactic)	Suggested Strategy (tactic)
Knowledge, skills, abilities Exhibit 11a	Directing Doris by going ON RECORD POLITELY: TENDING AUTONOMY NEEDS (Be Impersonal) *Effort must be made in the verification and filing of Form 3s...*	Go OFF RECORD (Be Cursory) instead: Delete message as it undermines rare praise and is included in another section. Or go ON RECORD PLAINLY (Be Explicit and Direct) instead: *I recommend that you proactively deal with verification and filing of Form 3s...*
Work Habits Exhibit 11b	Valuing Doris by going ON RECORD POLITELY: TENDING AUTONOMY NEEDS (Be Deferential) *Although your job duties are mostly repetitive...I can depend on you...*	Go ON RECORD PLAINLY (Be Explicit and Direct and Be Brief) instead: *You are very dependable, showing up and contributing...*
	Directing Doris by going ON RECORD PLAINLY (Be Explicit and Direct) *Do not take a defensive stance when constructive criticism....*	Go OFF RECORD (Be Cursory) instead: Delete message as it undermines rare praise and is included in another section.
Judgment Exhibit 11c	Valuing Doris by going ON RECORD POLITELY: TENDING AUTONOMY NEEDS (Be Impersonal) *Little intervention is needed from me when you encounter some issues but some issues could be prevented with proactive measures...* Or Directing Doris by going ON RECORD POLITELY: TENDING EGO NEEDS	Go ON RECORD PLAINLY (Be Brief) instead if valuing: *I appreciate that you handle the majority of issues without intervention...* Or go ON RECORD PLAINLY (Be Explicit and Direct) instead if directing: *Develop a proactive plan which we can discuss.* Or Go OFF RECORD (Be Cursory) instead if directing: Delete message as it undermines rare praise and is included in another section.

Table 11b. Analysis of Mr. Russell's evaluation of Doris Johnson.

In the section of the evaluation reproduced in Exhibit 11b, Mr. Russell compliments Doris in an "underhanded" way. (I think we would categorize his communication strategy as ON RECORD POLITELY: TENDING AUTONOMY NEEDS but that seems strange since I don't perceive him as "polite" in this instance. However, his meaning is less clear than ON RECORD PLAINLY and clearer than OFF RECORD, so I think ON RECORD POLITELY is the logical choice. I guess he "mitigated" the positive effects in his message.) In any case, because a compliment will affect Doris' ego needs positively, it should be communicated as clearly as possible (see Table 11a)—especially because there is so much of the evaluation that will affect Doris negatively. To accomplish this communication strategy, Mr. Russell needs to get rid of all unneeded information (use the ON RECORD PLAINLY tactics, as shown in the Table 11b).

In that same section of the evaluation, Mr. Russell directs Doris using the ON RECORD PLAINLY strategy (*do not take a defensive stance...*). As with the initial section of the report, I think the leader would interact more as a leader if he used the OFF RECORD strategy and simply omitted this directive since it is repeated elsewhere in this performance evaluation. If fact, this is the kind of ego-threatening comment that should be delivered in a face-to-face medium, which is more supportive of the member's ego needs.

I believe the primary management action is ambiguous in the section of the evaluation in Exhibit 11c. On the one hand, Mr. Russell may be attempting to voice his appreciation for one of Doris' (few) strong points. If that is the leader's primary goal, then he should opt for a clearer ON RECORD PLAINLY strategy for communicating Doris' value (*I appreciate that you handle...*) and possibly omit his ego-threatening comment about the member being proactive. If, on the other hand, Mr. Russell is primarily interested in his organization goal (directing Doris to be more proactive), then he should go ON RECORD PLAINLY with his directive. The leader successfully adopts that strategy when issuing the final directives in this section of the evaluation (*do not wait until the situation...* and *come to me with recommendations...*).

In conclusion, I have to say that, although Mr. Russell can demonstrate more ability to interact like a leader by changing some communication strategies in this performance evaluation, some face-to-face communication would be required to tend Doris' ego needs in this management situation.

Application 12A

In this management situation, Rubin wanted to maximize output by directing Norma in how to behave with the other members of the union organization (especially Peter). Because Rubin intervenes on behalf of Peter by chastising Norma for her treatment of a fellow volunteer, Rubin's actions are clearly threatening to both Norma's ego and autonomy needs.

Rubin reacts to Norma's attack on Peter with two predominantly ON RECORD PLAINLY Messages: *Norma, shut your cake hole* and *Now get the hell outta the office*. His use of the imperative form for both makes his intended action of directing Norma's behavior explicit. In addition, he uses the Be First tactic by beginning his interaction with these directives. Finally, he uses the Be Brief tactic by saying nothing more to Norma (except *Out* which is a shortened form of another imperative) while she remains in the office—even when she attempts to defend herself. The only thing about these two messages that is not plain is the use of slang (*cake hole*). Because slang is consistent with Norma's own verbal behavior (as we see later in their interaction), Rubin's choice here could be seen as TENDING EGO NEEDS by using in-group markers.

Rubin begins their interaction a few minutes later in the restaurant by informing Norma why he removed her from the office going ON RECORD PLAINLY (i.e., *Mouthy . . . you're too muscular. You can't come down that hard on a man and leave him his balls. Easy*). However, Rubin's intention throughout the rest of their interaction is to make clear how much he values Norma within their organization. In fact, Rubin's appearance at the restaurant was a signal that he valued her. He uses the OFF RECORD tactic of listening (i.e., *uh huh*) while she explains her behavior (i.e., *cotton mill workers is known as trash to some. . .*). He tends Norma's ego needs ON RECORD PLAINLY by comparing her to a great leader concisely, with no unneeded information (i.e., *our own Mother Jones*). He goes ON RECORD POLITELY: TENDING EGO NEEDS when calling her *kid* (the Be Inclusive tactic).

All of these behaviors in the restaurant showed that Rubin valued Norma and wanted to attend to their relationship after he chose to privilege the organization's needs over hers back at the office. Rubin's intent was to build commitment and organizational trust, and judging by Norma's joking behavior at the end of their interaction, Rubin had managed his relationship with her effectively even in this rapport-threatening management situation. This interaction could only be successful between a leader and an in-group member, someone with whom the leader has excellent rapport and whom the leader is certain desires candor.

Index

N

O

P

Q

R

S

T

U

Z